salad dress.
p 57

TASTING GOLD

A Goldmine of Recipes from Nevada County's Best Restaurants

TASTING GOLD

A Goldmine of Recipes from Nevada County's Best Restaurants

SUSAN WOLBARST
with Photos by Hank Meals

PUBLISHED BY SUSAN WOLBARST
13010 FROSTY LANE, GRASS VALLEY, CA 95945

DESIGNED AND PRODUCED BY DAVE COMSTOCK
PRINTED AND BOUND BY THOMSON-SHORE, INC.
ON RECYCLED ACID-FREE PAPER
LIBRARY OF CONGRESS CATALOG CARD NUMBER 92-90773

COVER PHOTOS BY HANK MEALS

This book is dedicated to my husband,
David Zachary Shpak.
His encouragement, patience, and support
consistently astonish me.

Contents

TRUCKEE

Acknowledgments

I OWE A GREAT DEAL to Nevada County's hard-working restaurateurs, many of them chefs, who generously shared their secret recipes. In addition, many served up appetizing lore about their buildings. Some chefs spent a great deal of time working with me, returning countless phone calls, answering questions and honing recipes to make them useful to home cooks.

Other people helped immensely with this project. At the top of the list is the ever-patient, generous, and good-humored Ed Tyson of Nevada County Historical Society's Searls Library. And Michel Janicot supplied valuable information about historic Grass Valley buildings now housing some of our county's best restaurants.

Thanks also to George Nelson, Dale Teubert and Rob Sayers for help filling in some historical gaps, and to the wonderful staff at the Nevada County Library for dependable, prompt, and friendly assistance.

I'm grateful to Dave Comstock for answering a million and a half questions about book making, publishing, design and distribution.

Many thanks to Patricia Hamilton and David Shpak for loaning me their sharp eyes, brains and stomachs. Not only did they come up with good pointers while editing, they also tasted many recipes in the book when I tested them. (And so did Henry Misrock, Susan Ellenbogen and Michael Miller.)

And I'd like to end with a word of appreciation to all the friends and family members who helped make this project happen.

Thanks.

Introduction

PEOPLE IN NEVADA COUNTY love to argue. No subject is mundane enough to be immune from disagreement and heated debate. So this book, like any printed opinion, will spawn arguments.

Fine. Go argue over a glass of wine and a good meal.

If I left out your brother-in-law's cousin's ex-wife's restaurant, it was probably because I had a lousy meal there. Or because an ingredient they list as "crab" on their menu isn't. Or maybe they had rotten service, a great way to sabotage even the finest meal.

Some restaurants were eliminated from consideration because they've proven inconsistent, serving a very nice meal on one visit followed by something quite different the next time. In many cases, these unpredictable places have suffered frequent owner-ship changes. Most of the restaurants described here feature very close "hands-on" supervision by owners, often doubling as chefs, who've kept up their track records for years.

Some restaurants couldn't be included because they declined to share recipes. That didn't dovetail with my idea of the book I wanted to put together.

As far as I know, no other book has been written about Nevada County's restaurants and their food. This may be because we're not exactly on the trendy circuit, where people with lots of money flock to spend it. Still, Nevada County has always had more good restaurants than one usually finds in an area of this population. Our restaurants are supported by tourists as well as locals earning wages characterized by what we call "the pine cone differential," i.e. low pay because this "desirable" place has fewer available jobs than job seekers. Many of us living here don't earn enough to eat out too often, which is why we're very selective when we do go out. It's also a reason I wanted to include recipes in this book.

Authors writing about Nevada County are more attracted to its history than its food. Even this book can't ignore the past, since most restaurants described here are located in historic buildings. So I included a "Peek at the Past" for each older building to provide a context for your hamburger.

Nevada County, I suspect, has always been a place where one can find good things to eat if one knows where to look. I'm sure the county's earliest inhabitants knew exactly where to get the tastiest acorns, pine nuts, blackberries, game, fish, wild plum, etc.

Their wealth (ample food, mild climate, scenic beauty) was stolen from them as miners seeking gold flooded the area, shadowed by bakers, brewers, vintners, cooks and others eager to make a living satisfying the miners' needs. Hotels, bakeries, and restaurants were built, burned down, and rebuilt to serve the hundreds and thousands who came here, searching.

Grass Valley, Nevada City and Truckee were built, along with countless other burgs which have long-since disappeared into rubble. As a reporter writing in the December 22, 1850 issue of the *Alta California,* a San Francisco newspaper, saw it: "The growth of Nevada [now called Nevada City] has been one of those wonders in California which have astonished the beholder, but it shows the uncertainty of all business which depends upon the mines in any particular location. It may be good today, but disappear to-morrow."

While things were good, restaurants and hotel dining rooms (and the grocers and others who supplied them) thrived, as we can extrapolate from advertising in early local newspapers. The ads give us an idea of what was cooking in Nevada County in the 1860s. Consider these:

"The largest and finest assortment of fancy cakes, confectionaries, nuts, raisins, etc. I have a wagon and will deliver every morning, in any part of the city, Boston Brown Bread, Graham Bread, Pies, Etc. Hot coffee at all Hours."—Julius Dreyfuss, United States Bakery, 48 Pine St., N.C. (in *The Morning Transcript,* 1861.)

"Game Suppers, Oysters, Lobsters, and the good things in the market, furnished at a moments (sic) notice, and got up in a style suited to the tastes of the greatest epicure . . . Meals at all hours."—Fashion Restaurant, Commercial St., N.C. (in *The Morning Transcript,* 1861.)

"On Tuesday, Thursday and Friday of each week a fine assortment of Fresh Fish including Flounders, Rock and Tom Cod, Smelts, Sea Bass, Sturgeon, Pike, Crabs, Oysters, Shrimps, Mussels, etc. Our arrangements are such that we can obtain Fresh Fish of all kinds from San Francisco on the most reasonable terms—delivering our Fish in Grass Valley inside of twenty hours from the Bay."—E.W. Noonan and Co. at the Centre Merket [sic] on Main St., G.V. (in *The Union,* 1866.)

"The undersigned keep a large supply of FAMILY VEGETABLES. Their stock is received daily, is always fresh and consists of the following articles: Fresh Butter, Fresh Eggs, Cabbage, Fruits, Prunes, Cheese, Onions, Potatoes, Apples, Oranges. Also — GAME and POULTRY constantly on hand. The lowest cash prices."—Washington Market, No. 10 Commercial St., N.C. (in *The Morning Transcript,* 1861.)

"Continually on hand, the best LIQUORS, WINES, ALES, ETC. OYSTERS IN EVERY STYLE. Served up at all times, Day or Night."—Harmonie Saloon, Main St., G.V. (in *The Union,* 1866.)

"I have engaged the services of one of the BEST CONFECTIONERS in the State of California, and am now fully prepared to MAKE all kinds of CAKE in the French style, which cannot be surpassed in Nevada [City], or elsewhere. I am always prepared to SUPPLY BALLS AND PARTIES with Confectionery of every variety, including Fancy Pound Cake, Spunge [sic] Cake, Raisins, etc."—Otto Lutje, Proprietor, Cheap Refreshment Saloon, 69 Broad St., N.C. (In *The Morning Transcript,* 1861.)

Since the 1850s, the county has seen boom times and busts, as its various industries (gold, timber, and—in Truckee—ice) have thrived, then floundered due to changing conditions beyond anyone's control. Many, many restaurants have come and gone, even in the 19 years I've lived here.

Restaurants which thrive do so on reputation. In small towns, the grapevine has always been the most potent (and sometimes deadly) form of advertising. The best restaurants earn the most worthwhile accolade: regular customers.

There is no particular "local cuisine" in Nevada County restaurants.[1] Instead, there are gifted and creative chefs providing their interpretations of what great food should taste like today in Grass Valley, Nevada City and Truckee. They borrow freely from the cooking of Mexico, Japan, Thailand, France (or even Philadelphia) to put the product they want on the table.

This book is to help the people who really care about food—those who define and remember a place by its steamed mussels and its cheesecake—spend their time and money judiciously in Nevada County, whether they're passing through or putting down roots here.

A restaurant, after all, is often a person's first "taste" of a place. And returning to a favorite restaurant for a familiar dish is, for me anyway, "going home." Changes in menu, atmosphere or prices can bring deep disappointment; an old favorite closing its doors is like a death.

Regrettably, some parts of the book could be out of date by the time you get your hands on it. (A standard line among acquaintances when I've described this project has been: "How many of the restaurants you're writing about have gone out of business since you started the book?" The answer, by the way, is none.) But the sad inevitablity is that even some of our "landmark" establishments (remember Pearl's Kozy Spot? Mama Su's?) eventually closed their doors, leaving devotees to moan and reminisce. The rhythm of economic life certainly won't change for anything as minor as publishing a book. I plan to offset this predictable inconvenience by updating the book periodically—annually if necessary—to keep the information current.

If I've left out your favorite restaurant, or included one where your experience was less than outstanding, I'd like to hear from you as part of my research for future editions. Please write to me at 13010 Frosty Lane, Grass Valley, CA 95945.

1. The one possible exception is the "Cornish Pastie." Several businesses around Nevada County sell these, and since they've been sufficiently romanticized in various newspaper and magazine articles, I won't trouble you with additional pastie lore. If you'd like to try one, I recommend Mrs. Dubblebee's Pasties at 251C South Auburn St., Grass Valley. I find the spinach-filled pasties far tastier than the traditional meat and potatoes types. Whichever you choose, let them heat it up for you and don't forget to douse generously with malt vinegar.

Now read, and prepare to hunker down to some great eating. Work up an appetite enjoying the history and the scenery. If you've come to Nevada County searching for good food, you won't be disappointed. And the recipes included here let you revisit Nevada County's best restaurants in your own kitchen, any time, anywhere.

TASTING GOLD IN GRASS VALLEY

Grass Valley's finest pastries and high octane
coffee in the dawn's early dark.

FLOUR GARDEN BAKERY

11999 Sutton Way, Grass Valley
☎ (916) 272-2043 and
109 Neal St., Grass Valley
☎ (916) 477-2253
Monday–Saturday: 5 a.m.–6 p.m.
Sunday: 6 a.m.–6 p.m.
Continental breakfast, some lunch items

Everything from scratch

COMMUTERS AND CONSTRUCTION WORKERS are waiting at 5 a.m. when the Flour Garden's doors open. A cup of high-octane Flour Garden coffee and some goody or other are bare essentials in the dawn's early light.

There's a bright cosmopolitan crispness to these white rooms: classical music, newspapers, smells of coffee and sweet temptation. If it's a quick breakfast you're after, or a fresh baguette and some cookies for your picnic, this is the place. They've got all the muffins, bagels, and Danish you can handle, as well as croissants stuffed with smoked turkey and Swiss cheese or spinach and provolone ($1.85) or chocolate. Their English Tea Scones (95 cents apiece) are heaven with strawberry jam and butter.

"The thing about the Flour Garden Bakery that makes it unique and special is that we make everything from scratch," says owner Susan Copeland. "We use great ingredients. The reason other bakeries don't do it is it's incredibly expensive in terms of labor and ingredients."

She estimates that ingredients used at Flour Garden cost three times as much as the mixes, buckets of frozen eggs, cheap oils, and other components used at most commercial bakeries. "Their blueberries are pieces of apple soaked in blue dye," she says. At Flour Garden, ingredients are listed in the bakery case beside each item.

Cookies, fruit custard tarts, and cakes sold at Flour Garden's three locations (there's another at Auburn Town Center) are top notch. As are the latest "healthy lunch" offerings, including

Spinach Ricotta Lasagna, Black Bean Polenta ($2.25 a slice), and quiches.

And the coffee here is not to be underestimated. Custom-roasted for Flour Garden in the Bay Area, its caffeine content is matched by excellent flavor. They also sell decaf, whatever that is.

A tag on a basket of their Sourdough Baguettes ($1.39 for a 1-pound loaf) boasts, "We want you to know this baguette is as excellent a baguette as you will find anywhere in the world! Buy two. One for the ride home and one for when you get home." Other breads offered on various days of the week include Garlic Twist, Savory Rosemary, Infinity, Jalapeño Cheesebread, and Tibetan Way ($1.50–$2.45 per loaf).

The Copelands brought their first Flour Garden to Nevada County in 1981. Susan's husband Bill, a builder, did all the plumbing, electrical, equipment installation, etc. at each of their stores. She has an art background, evident in the silk-screened irises and other decoration.

Flour Garden Bakery
Danish Butternuts/Mexican Wedding Cookies

"These butter cookies are great for sending as gifts—they travel and last well."—Susan Copeland

3 cups (1½ pounds) butter
¾ cup powdered sugar, plus extra for coating
   finished cookies
6 tablespoons vanilla extract
2 cups walnut pieces
3¾ cups unbleached all-purpose flour

Blend butter and sugar together minimally. Then blend in other ingredients. Do not overmix. Dough should be stiff. Scoop dough into balls with a spoon. Round them up with your hands. Bake at 325 degrees until golden brown, about 30–45 minutes. Cool. When COMPLETELY cooled, roll them in powdered sugar, covering them completely. (Makes 2–3 dozen.)

Chad Wadsworth, Flour Garden Bakery.

Flour Garden Bakery Irish Soda Bread

"An unusual and richly flavorful bread with its combination of caraway and whiskey-soaked dried fruits. A favorite here in the Foothills with its many descendants of Irish miners."—Susan Copeland

>   1½ cups raisins
>   1 cup dried peaches, cut into chunks
>   ½ cup Irish whiskey
>   5 cups whole wheat flour
>   5 cups whole wheat pastry flour
>   4 teaspoons baking soda
>   1 tablespoon salt
>   2 tablespoons caraway seeds
>   ¼ cup honey or brown sugar
>   1 pound (2 cups) butter or margarine
>   5 cups buttermilk

Place whiskey in a small bowl. Soak raisins and peaches in whiskey until they are soft and saturated with liquor. Set aside. Blend remaining dry ingredients in a large bowl. Then cut the butter into the flour mixture, using a pastry blender, as you would for biscuits—until the butter is in pea-sized pieces, but not completely blended into the dough. Then add the dried fruits, whiskey and buttermilk (also the honey, if you're using it instead of brown sugar.) Blend until the dough is uniformly wet, but not smooth. Divide dough into six portions. Lightly knead the dough, shaping it gently into round loaves. Slice a cross in the top of each—not too deeply—for decoration. Place loaves on a lightly greased baking sheet and bake at 350 degrees until golden brown, about 30–45 minutes. (Makes six loaves. Susan says you can halve this recipe to make less bread, and extra loaves store well in the freezer.)

Flour Garden Bakery Snickerdoodles

6¼ cups plus 2 tablespoons of sugar
1¾ cups butter
2 cups vegetable shortening
¾ cup margarine
10 eggs
4¼ cups unbleached white pastry flour
2½ tablespoons cream of tartar
¾ tablespoon salt
2 tablespoons baking soda
4¼ cups unbleached all-purpose flour
cinnamon and sugar for sprinkling

Cream first four ingredients together until light and fluffy. Then whip in the eggs. Sift together the dry ingredients and slowly add to the creamed mixture. Blend thoroughly. Scoop the finished cookie dough with a spoon or small scoop, placing small balls of dough onto lightly greased (or covered with baking parchment) cookie sheets. Before baking, sprinkle each cookie with cinnamon and sugar. Bake in 350-degree oven until cookies are golden brown around the edges, about 12–15 minutes. (Makes six dozen.)

Flour Garden Bakery Tibetan Way Bread

"This is a dense, hearty bread—very nutritious. Great for hiking or serving sliced thin with a ripe brie or other flavorful cheese. It is low in oil, yeast and salt. No eggs. Dairy is optional."—Susan Copeland

> **4 cups water**
> **1 ounce (2 tablespoons) yeast**
> **¾ cup barley flour**
> **2½ cups coarse whole wheat flour, plus more
>   for kneading**
> **4 tablespoons honey**
> **1½ cups coarse cornmeal**
> **1¾ cups millet**
> **1½ cups dates**
> **½ cup corn oil**
> **1 tablespoon sea salt**
> **½ cup nonfat dry milk**

Blend the first five ingredients in large bowl. Cover the bowl and place in a warm, draft-free spot and allow the sponge to double in size. Then blend in the remaining ingredients. Knead the dough, using whole wheat flour as needed to keep the dough from being too sticky. When dough is well-kneaded, it will be heavy, but not stiff. Form into five round loaves, cover, and allow them to rise in a warm place until almost double in size. Then bake at 325 degrees for about an hour. Bread is done when a loaf sounds hollow when tapped on the bottom. (Recipe makes five loaves. It can be cut for smaller quantity with no ill effects, Susan says, and extra loaves keep well in the freezer.)

**Flour Garden's daily harvest
includes scones and muffins.**

9

GOLD STAR CAFE*

207 West Main St., Grass Valley
☎ **(916) 477-1523**
Wednesday–Friday: 7:30 a.m.–2 p.m.
Saturday–Sunday: 8 a.m.–2 p.m.
Breakfast and lunch
✌ **Reservations suggested during peak hours**

Tastiest breakfasts in Western Nevada County

DENISE WILSON, who owns the Gold Star Cafe with her musician husband, Peter, uses only fresh ingredients and makes everything from scratch. Her talents in her postage stamp kitchen pack this small place with customers, many of them "regulars" who eat here every day.

"A lot of cooks hate cooking breakfast, because there's too much going on. To me it's the easiest thing there is. I like the pace—it never stops," Denise says.

The Gold Star serves breakfast all day. There's also a lunch menu with burgers, salads, soup and sandwiches, including interesting choices for vegetarians such as a Tempeh Burger with grilled onions and lime horseradish mayo ($4.50) or Pesto Pizza on Roll ($4.75) featuring olive oil, garlic, red onion, tomato, cheese, pesto sauce, and black olives baked on a roll.

Gold Star breakfasts are so good, however, that many customers have never tried the lunches. Some never even get around to reading the menu, because the daily specials on the blackboard are always too seductive to pass up. These may include Blueberry Pancakes with real maple syrup or a Bay Shrimp Scramble

*__Note:__ As this book goes to press, the Gold Star appears, sadly, about ready to ascend to Restaurant Heaven. An escrow is progressing, and the Gold Star Cafe may be history by the time you read this. If you never had the pleasure of sampling Denise's wonderful cooking, the recipes included here are your only chance to get a taste of what you missed. The rest of us will have to bite the bullet and cook our own Gold Star meals, lamenting our tragic loss.

11

(scrambled eggs with shrimp, sun-dried tomatoes, marinated artichoke hearts, garlic, basil, and feta cheese.)

Choices from the menu include the Breakfast Quesadilla, a flour tortilla filled with scrambled eggs, green chilies, avocado, black olives, and green onion, topped with sour cream and salsa. Or crepes topped with olallieberries, or Greek Baked Eggs (two eggs baked with spinach, onion, black olives, feta and jack cheese.)

Portions are quite generous, so don't eat breakfast here at noon and plan on going out to dinner at 6. Chances are, you won't be hungry.

In summer, you may choose to eat outside on the back patio. You'll be surrounded by old brick buildings with huge iron shutters and corrugated metal siding: a raw taste of Grass Valley's fire-plagued past.

At the Gold Star, your check is served with little star-shaped cookies for everyone at the table. The only problem is that you may be too full to eat them.

PEEK AT THE PAST

The Gold Star Cafe is located in The Beatty House-Quick Building, which spans 205–209 West Main Street. According to research by Grass Valley author and historian Michel Janicot, a wooden frame hotel-boarding house built on this site in late 1850 by Thomas and Zacheus Beatty served as Grass Valley's second hostelry. (The first was The Mountain House, built of logs on Mill Street in September, 1850.) Destroyed by fire in 1855, it was rebuilt of wood. The present two-story brick structure was built in the early 1920s.

In 1882, A. P. Tietje and his brother Henry opened a cigar factory on the site, using "the best Havana tobacco" with "none but White Labor employed." A third brother, Dietrich, succeeded them in 1883 and ran the business for two years, then took William Parsons as a partner in the manufacture of "the Sierra Nevada Cigar." Parsons married Lavigna Quick in 1885 and by 1887 had acquired a new partner—Paul Quick—his father-in-law.

The building contained a barber shop for some 20–30 years, until the 1970s, when it became the Aldebaran Cafe.

Gold Star Cafe Bay Shrimp Scramble

1 teaspoon butter
¼ teaspoon crushed garlic
6 to 8 marinated artichoke hearts
8 sun-dried tomatoes, packed in oil
½ cup bay shrimp, thawed
pinch of dry basil
¼ cup feta cheese
4 eggs, beaten
minced fresh parsley for garnish

Sauté garlic in butter. Add artichokes, tomatoes, bay shrimp and basil. Sauté lightly until completely warmed. Set aside. Put beaten eggs in a warm, lightly buttered omelet pan. Scramble until soft. Add shrimp mixture, fold, then add feta. Sprinkle with minced fresh parsley and serve. (Serves two.)

Finish to another stellar meal.

Gold Star Cafe Croissant French Toast

2 large day-old croissants
4 eggs
¼ cup heavy cream
dash of nutmeg
¼ teaspoon sugar
Orange Olallieberry Sauce (recipe follows),
    jam or maple syrup

Slice croissants in half lengthwise. Set aside. Break eggs into blender and beat. Add cream, nutmeg, and sugar to eggs, blend well. Pour mixture into a shallow bowl. Submerge croissants in egg mixture and fry on preheated griddle or skillet until golden brown. Serve with Orange Olallieberry Sauce, jam or maple syrup. (Serves two.)

Gold Star Cafe Orange Olallieberry Sauce

1 cup frozen olallieberries (or raspberries, or
    boysenberries)
¼ cup maple syrup
¼ cup fresh orange juice
1 tablespoon cornstarch
grated zest of one orange

Cook berries lightly in saucepan to release juice. Add syrup and orange juice, stirring. Dissolve cornstarch in a small amount of water. Add to sauce to thicken. Stir in zest of orange just before serving. (If you have leftover sauce, Denise says it will keep in the refrigerator for up to a week.)

Gold Star Cafe Greek Baked Eggs

For each serving:
- 1/2 teaspoon butter
- 1 tablespoon finely chopped red onion
- 1/8 teaspoon crushed garlic
- 1 cup cleaned spinach leaves
- 1 tablespoon black olives, sliced
- 2 eggs
- 1 tablespoon feta cheese, crumbled
- 2 tablespoons Monterey jack, grated

Preheat oven to 375 degrees. Melt butter and lightly sauté the onion, garlic, and spinach. Place in a ramekin or other small individual baking dish. Add olives. Crack eggs into baking dish on top of spinach mixture and olives. Sprinkle with feta and Monterey jack. Bake 10 to 20 minutes.

Denise Wilson, Gold Star's owner and chef.

Gold Star Cafe Muffins

Note: Begin these the day before you plan to serve them. They need to sit in the refrigerator overnight before baking.

2 eggs	½ tablespoon
1½ cups sugar	cinnamon
½ cup canola oil	dash nutmeg
3 cups unbleached white	½ teaspoon salt
flour	2 cups milk
1 tablespoon baking soda	2 cups whole oats
1 tablespoon baking	1 cup baker's bran
powder	1 cup water

Mix eggs, sugar, and oil. Add flour, baking soda, baking powder, cinnamon, nutmeg, salt and milk, then stir. Add oats, bran and water. Stir well. Let sit overnight (or up to 4 days) in refrigerator. When ready to bake, mix in fruit, nuts, etc. using the following list (or your own substitutions. "You can put anything in these," according to Denise.) Oil the muffin tins and fill them fairly full, then bake at 350 degrees for 20–30 minutes. Makes two dozen.

Variations:

For Apple Walnut Muffins: Add 1 or 2 grated apples and 1 cup chopped walnuts.

For Banana Nut Muffins: Add 2 large ripe bananas, mashed and 1 cup chopped walnuts or pecans.

For Orange Poppy Seed Muffins: Add the grated zest of 2 oranges and 2 or 3 tablespoons of poppy seeds.

For Pumpkin Muffins: Add one cup of pumpkin purée and ½ teaspoon allspice.

For Pear Pecan Muffins: Add 1 or 2 chopped pears and 1 cup chopped pecans.

For Chocolate Walnut Muffins: Add ½ to 1 cup chocolate chips and 1 cup chopped walnuts.

For Sweet Potato Muffins: Add 1 cup puréed sweet potatoes and ½ teaspoon allspice.

For Peach Muffins: Add 2 or 3 fresh peaches, chopped.

Gold Star Cafe Pesto Garden Frittata

1 tablespoon butter
1 medium carrot, grated
1 cup sliced mushrooms
1/3 cup chopped gold bell pepper
1/2 pound chopped spinach
1/3 cup chopped red onion
3 large cloves garlic, chopped
5 tablespoons homemade or frozen pesto sauce
5 eggs, beaten

Preheat oven to 375 degrees. Melt butter. Sauté the vegetables in a very large cast-iron skillet. Add pesto sauce. Add eggs* and bake in preheated oven 20 to 25 minutes. (Serves four.)

Note: If your skillet isn't big enough, transfer the vegetables and pesto sauce to a large baking dish, then add the eggs and bake.

The ARLETTA DOUGLAS ROOM

THE HOLBROOKE
212 Main Street, Grass Valley
☎ (916) 273-1353; (800) 933-7077
Lunch Monday–Friday, 11 a.m.–2 p.m.;
Dinner Monday–Saturday 5:30 p.m.–9 p.m.;
Sunday Brunch 10 a.m.–2 p.m.
♆ Reservations recommended

Black Bart ate here (maybe)

THE HOLBROOKE RESTAURANT, located inside "Grass Valley's Grand Hotel," is worth visiting not only for a tasty meal, but to soak up the flavor of Grass Valley back when the town's name was synonymous with big bucks from the gold mines.

Painstaking restoration of the Holbrooke has given Grass Valley residents a landmark to be proud of, and the elegant authority of the surroundings makes a worthwhile backdrop for lunch, Sunday brunch or dinner.

You enter the main dining room through a pair of massive brick arches. Exposed brick the length of two walls, complimented by a dark green patterned rug and floral curtains, help make this one of the most attractive dining rooms in the Gold Country.

The recently revised dinner menu includes appetizers like steamed clams, escargots, spinach linguini, or a Hot Dungeness Crab concoction which includes artichoke hearts, Parmesan cheese and onions, served with sourdough bread. Appetizer prices average about $7.

Samples of entrées you might want to consider for dinner: Chicken Chardonnay (chicken breast stuffed with crab, shrimp, shallots, capers and bread crumbs, topped with wine sauce and served with grapes), a char-broiled Filet Mignon wrapped with bacon and served with Danish blue cheese sauce or Pacific Salmon teamed with peaches and cranberries in a mustard cream sauce. Other entrées offer a lot of variety: Creole Sauté (chicken, prawns and andouille sausage with peppers, onions, tomatoes

19

and garlic), Prime Rib on Friday and Saturday nights, T-Bone steak with bourbon peppercorn sauce.

Prices are in the $15–$18 range, including soup or salad, potatoes or rice, vegetables and hot sourdough bread. Portions are quite generous.

Those who prefer pasta will find several choices, including a fresh linguini topped with prosciutto, mushrooms and brandy pesto cream sauce ($12.) Tempting salads include The Holbrooke's delicious version of a Caesar and a roasted marinated chicken breast accompanied by candied pecans, goat cheese and flowering kale with a balsamic vinegar, Dijon mustard, fresh thyme dressing ($7.)

Desserts include a Hazelnut Chocolate Cake which won a blue ribbon at the 1986 Nevada County Fair, Kahlua Chocolate Mousse, and Apple Strudel served warm with caramel sauce and crème anglaise. Daily dessert specials are offered, often including old-fashioned Bread Pudding jazzed up with Whiskey Sauce.

For lunch, choose from a lengthy list of salads, sandwiches, burgers, pasta and four specials a day. Thursday is Mexican Day at The Holbrooke, with appropriate lunchtime items borrowed from that cuisine. Lunch prices average $6.

Work up a good appetite hiking around Grass Valley's hills before attempting the $11.95 ($7.95 for children) brunch on Sunday. This all-you-can-eat bonanza features items like cold red trout with dill, potato pancakes, pork loin, quiches, linguisa scramble, biscuits, sausage, deli salads, carrot cake, cinnamon rolls, and more. All the champagne or sparkling apple cider you can drink is included.

While visiting the Holbrooke, be sure to check out the bar, also known as the Golden Gate Saloon. It has copper walls on three sides, huge arches, lots of glass (including a great view of the unusual glass and wrought iron sided elevator and whoever might be riding it) and a mahogany bar with a stained glass legend: "Golden Gate Saloon—est. 1852."

Food and drinks can also be enjoyed on The Holbrooke's patio in nice weather. Other amenities: three banquet rooms seating 40–85 for private gatherings, 17 hotel rooms in the main building and 9 more in the adjacent Purcell House, ample parking behind the hotel, occasional weekend comedy and live music ("blues in the bar").

PEEK AT THE PAST

Four U.S. Presidents (Grant, Harrison, Garfield and Cleveland), writers Mark Twain and Bret Harte, champion heavyweight boxers Jim Corbett and Bob Fitzsimmons, and the outlaw Black Bart are among the famous guests who've visited Grass Valley's Holbrooke Hotel. You can see some of their names in the guest book displayed in the lobby.

The Holbrooke was originally built in 1851 as two buildings: the Golden Gate Saloon and the Adams Express Office. Both wooden structures, they were destroyed in the 1855 fire which consumed most of Grass Valley. Stephen Smith rebuilt the Golden Gate in 1856 as a one-story fieldstone building with a brick facade. Until it was closed briefly in 1989, the Golden Gate Saloon was reputed to be the oldest continuously operating saloon in the state.

In 1862, a relative of Stephen named Charles Smith built the present structure, calling it the Exchange Hotel and incorporating the saloon into the building. Like other historic Grass Valley buildings, it was fortified against fire with heavy iron doors, brick, and a foot-deep layer of dirt or broken brick on the roof. It's not clear whether these precautions were put in place before or after the August 15, 1862 fire. Describing that fire in their 1880 *History of Nevada County,* publishers Thompson and West reported: "The Exchange Hotel, a new building but partly finished, was on fire several times, but was saved from destruction."

Charles Smith sold the hotel in 1877 to M. P. O'Connor, who sold it two years later to Ellen and Daniel P. Holbrooke. Daniel died in 1884, but Mrs. Holbrooke continued to manage the hotel until 1908. That year, The Holbrooke was purchased at public auction by Elizabeth and Oeter Johnson. In 1922, it was inherited by their daughters, Lily J. Cory and Sadie P. Finnie. It passed to Sadie's husband Robert in 1947, and was sold to Emma and Harold Moneyhun in 1954.

The next owner, Arletta Douglas, began a major rehabilitation of the building in 1972, including restoration of the original arches and staircases. Richard Kline bought the Holbrooke in

1980, completing the refurbishing in 1982 and acquiring the nearby Purcell House (119 North Church Street) the following year. The Purcell House was built in 1874 as a home for Peter Purcell and his family, who operated the nearby Fashion Livery Stable. The Purcell House was restored for use as a bed and breakfast inn in 1981.

The Holbrooke's executive chef, David Silverman, with Chicken Chardonnay.

The Holbrooke Chicken Chardonnay

4 boneless chicken breasts, skin removed
small amount of olive oil

For stuffing:

4 ounces Dungeness crabmeat
4 ounces bay shrimp
2 ounces bread crumbs
1 teaspoon chopped fresh shallots
1 teaspoon capers
1 egg
salt and pepper to taste

For sauce:

1 cup chardonnay
½ teaspoon chopped shallots
1 cup cream
2 ounces butter
green seedless grapes, for garnish

Pound the chicken breasts flat. Combine stuffing ingredients well and divide into four portions. Place one portion on each breast and roll into a tube. Place rolled breasts in a baking dish, seam side down, and rub each with a small amount of olive oil. Roast in a 450-degree oven until done, approximately 20–25 minutes.

While breasts are cooking, make the sauce. Place chardonnay and shallots in a saucepan and boil until reduced by one-half. Add cream and reduce again, this time by one-third. Swirl in 2 ounces of butter just before serving.

To serve, slice the finished breasts into medallions with stuffing in the center. Place 1½ ounces of sauce on each plate and arrange medallions on sauce. Garnish with grapes. (Serves four.)

The Holbrooke Hot Dungeness Crab Appetizer

6 ounces Dungeness crabmeat
6 ounces chopped artichoke hearts
3 ounces grated Parmesan cheese
3 ounces thinly sliced onions
1⅓ cups mayonnaise
1 large sourdough baguette, sliced
1 tablespoon chopped fresh parsley

Preheat oven to 400 degrees. Combine first four ingredients with mayonnaise. Place one-fourth of the mixture in each of four oven-proof individual baking dishes. Cook 8–10 minutes, until the mixture is bubbly. Arrange sliced bread on each plate around the dip and garnish with fresh parsley. (Serves four.)

Grass Valley's handsomest landmark.

Copper walls reflect the light inside the
Golden Gate Saloon at the Holbrooke.

MAIN STREET
RESTAURANT
WINE·GIFTS·CHOCOLATE·GELATO
RESTAURANT

MAIN STREET CAFE

213 West Main Street, Grass Valley
☎ **(916) 477-6000**
Lunch: Monday–Friday, 11:30 a.m.–3 p.m.;
Saturday, noon–3 p.m.
Dinner: Sunday–Thursday, 5 p.m.–9 p.m.;
Friday and Saturday, 5 p.m.–10 p.m.
✌ **Reservations suggested**

Finely-crafted food, relaxed setting

RICHARD AND CAROL BUCKLEY bought this aging building in 1978 and transformed it into Main Street Cafe, which he describes as "the place we always wanted to go to that wasn't there. What we wanted was a place where we could be comfortable and get great food and a glass of wine. There wasn't one."

Buckley, a former manager of Dingus McGee's in Colfax, was soon joined by former Dingus chef Robert Gallegos. They've succeeded in cooking up a cozy cafe which offers consistently flavorful meals.

Dinner entrées are served with bread and butter, red beans and rice, vegetable, and soup or salad. If I can offer three words of advice: try the Scampi. I find myself returning to Main Street again and again for this superb dish, and I'm really pleased that Robert offered his recipe for this book. Red beans and rice make the perfect compliment.

Another popular specialty is Blackened Filet with Crawfish Étouffée, in which the beef is blackened with spices, then topped with a Cajun stew of crawfish tails and green onion. Other possibilities include Chicken in Lime and Cilantro served over a Lime Hollandaise, or Ginger Prawns and Scallops sautéed with broccoli, peanuts and soy sauce. Entrées range $10.95–$17.95.

Richard Buckley found his favorite
restaurant the hard way—he built it.

27

Those drawn to pasta will find a couple of unusual combinations (as well as Fettucini Alfredo and other standards) like the Sausage with Fettucini al Pesto, which teams spicy Italian sausage with olive oil, fresh sweet basil, cream and green apple. Or the Filet Primavera with Lemon-Basil Fettucini, in which strips of filet mignon are sautéed with vegetables, blended with veal sauce and served on fresh lemon-basil fettucini, garnished with freshly grated Parmesan. Pasta dishes average $12.

Appetizers include grilled Wild Boar Sausage on a bed of applesauce, Tempura Veggies, and seafood specials like Oysters on the Half-Shell or Lemon Grass Mussels. Appetizers average about $6.

There are some very potent temptations offered here in the dessert category, such as Bailey's Irish Cream Cheesecake, Mississippi Mud Cake and Chocolate Turtle Torte.

A separate bar menu is available for the adjacent bar, featuring unusual "Gourmet Pizzas" in flavors like Southern Crawfish Bar-B-Que; Smoked Trout with Lemon; and Artichokes, Pesto and 3 Cheeses (mozzarella, Parmesan and provolone.) Other offerings are appetizers and desserts from the restaurant menu, plus "Light Fare" like Hot Thai Chicken Salad and Pesto Chicken Burger. Prices range $5.95–$7.95.

For lunch, they've got "Gourmet Burgers" (beef, chicken, veggie and—for those hankering for something Old-Westish—a Buffalo Burger makes frequent appearances as a special.) Or you may be attracted to homemade soup and a salad, or the "Salad Sampler," which lets you try the pasta salad, chicken tarragon salad and shrimp salad.

Several kinds of pasta are served for lunch, including the tasty Ravioli Pesto, filled with ricotta and spinach and served with a pesto cream sauce and Parmesan, as well as a green salad.

Both cold and hot sandwiches are available. An example is the Hot Turkey Laredo, with roasted turkey breast, jack cheese, guacamole, sour cream and salsa. Lunch prices range from $4.75 to $7.25.

Drinks or meals can be enjoyed on the patio in nice weather.

PEEK AT THE PAST

Main Street Cafe is located on the site of William K. Spencer's stationery store and telegraph office, opened some time after September, 1855. (Spencer had an earlier location behind the Holbrooke Hotel, which burned along with virtually the entire town in the disastrous fire of September 13, 1855. Only two businesses survived the blaze, which consumed more than 300 structures on 30 acres.)

But to Grass Valley old-timers, this location will always be described as "the old OK Pool Hall," a business which lasted from approximately the 1920s into the 1970s. In 1973, Dale Teubert maintained a bit of pool-playing but converted the ambiance when he opened The Hardrock Saloon on the site. Named for the area's hardrock mining, the place is fondly re-membered by those of us who arrived here about then and gravitated to The Hardrock as a haven of imported beers and "foosball" games as well as pool. Dale sold the place in 1978, and a restaurant appeared there very briefly before the current owners took charge.

The Main Street Cafe's bar is located in the Van Hoeter Building, named for Pauline[1] and Joseph Van Hoeter, who owned the building as early as 1862. The couple successfully ran a soap factory for a number of years, as well as being involved in real estate and mining enterprises. By 1879, the building was candy factory. The Sanborn map of Grass Valley in 1898 shows it as "Tamale Kitchen." According to the late Frank Knuckey and Lloyd Veale, the building was home to the Jack O'Lantern Restaurant in the 1930s and 40s, and from 1948–1960 it housed "The Exclusive Beauty Shop." Next the Uptown Cafe and Happy Valley Cafe took up residence there, and in the early 70s, Nature's Way health foods store leased the premises.

---

1. Off the subject, but of historical interest, is that in 1890 Pauline Van Hoeter built and managed what was known as Van's Opera House at the present location of Hedman Furniture on Mill Street.

Main Street Bailey's Irish Cream Cheesecake

(Can be prepared a day ahead of serving, if desired.)

Crust:

10 whole graham crackers, broken into pieces
1¼ cups pecans (about 5 ounces)
¼ cup sugar
6 tablespoons (¾ stick) unsalted butter, melted

Filling:

1½ pounds cream cheese, at room temperature
¾ cup sugar
3 large eggs
⅓ cup Bailey's Original Irish Cream liqueur
1 teaspoon vanilla extract
3 ounces imported white chocolate (such as
    Lindt), broken in pieces

Topping:

1½ cups sour cream
¼ cup powdered sugar
1½ ounces imported white chocolate, grated
24 pecan halves

For crust: Lightly butter a 9-inch diameter springform pan with 2¾-inch tall sides. Finely grind graham crackers, pecans and sugar in food processor. Add butter and blend, using on/off turns. Press crumbs onto bottom and two inches up the sides of prepared pan. Refrigerate 20 minutes.

For filling: Using electric mixer, beat cream cheese and sugar in large bowl until smooth. In a separate medium-size bowl, whisk eggs, Bailey's and vanilla until just blended. Beat egg mixture into cream cheese mixture. Finely chop white chocolate in food processor, using on/off turns. Add to cream cheese mixture.

Preheat oven to 325 degrees. Transfer filling to crust-lined pan. Bake until edges of filling are puffed and dry-looking and center is just set, about 50 minutes. Cool on rack.

For topping: Mix sour cream and powdered sugar in small bowl.

Spread topping onto cooled cake. Refrigerate until well chilled, about 6 hours.

Sprinkle grated chocolate over cake. Place pecans around edge and serve. (Serves ten.)

Bailey's Irish Cream Cheesecake is a Main Street specialty.

Main Street Cafe Black Bean Soup

2 tablespoons olive oil
2 medium onions, chopped
6 stalks celery, chopped
3 cloves garlic, chopped
10–12 cups chicken stock
2 cups dry black beans
$\frac{1}{4}$ teaspoon cayenne pepper
juice of $\frac{1}{2}$ lemon
1 tablespoon lemon zest
$\frac{1}{4}$ teaspoon ground cloves
salt to taste
thinly sliced lemon, sour cream, chopped chives
    for garnish

In a large soup pot, add oil, onions, celery and garlic. Sauté until aromas rise and the vegetables are barely beginning to soften. Add stock, beans and the remaining ingredients (except garnish.) Boil for 2–4 hours until beans are done. Check periodically and add more stock if soup becomes dry. Serve with garnish of lemon wheels and/or sour cream and chopped chives. (Serves six to eight.)

Main Street Cafe Mulligatawny Soup

3 tablespoons olive oil
8 stalks celery, chopped
4 carrots, chopped
2 medium onions, chopped
1 small green bell pepper, chopped
1 small red bell pepper, chopped
4 cloves garlic, chopped
2 tablespoons fresh
    (or 1 tablespoon dried) oregano
2 tablespoons fresh
    (or 1 tablespoon dried) thyme
4–6 tablespoons Madras-style curry powder
1 bay leaf
1/4 teaspoon ground cloves
1 tablespoon crushed whole fennel seed
10–12 cups chicken stock
roux made with 1/4 pound margarine
    or butter and 1/4 cup flour
1 cup cream

In a large soup pot, place olive oil, celery, onions, carrots, bell peppers and garlic. Sauté lightly. As the vegetables begin to soften, add remaining ingredients, except the roux and the cream, and bring to a boil. Boil for 20 minutes.

Make the roux by melting margarine or butter, then adding flour, stirring continuously to make a thin paste. Add roux to the soup and boil for two minutes. Add cream and serve. (Serves six to eight.)

Main Street Orange-Gingered Pork Salad

6 ounces pork tenderloin, cut in thin strips and
   lightly floured
2 tablespoons olive oil
½ tablespoon chopped fresh ginger
½ tablespoon chopped fresh garlic
8 ounces port wine
10 mandarin orange segments (canned)
2 tablespoons mandarin orange juice (from can)
8 long thin slices of red bell pepper
8–10 pods snow peas
2 tablespoons bottled Chinese oyster sauce
4 cups salad greens, washed, dried and torn in
   bite-sized pieces

Brown pork tenderloin in olive oil. Add ginger and garlic and lightly sauté until aromas rise. Add port and boil until reduced by one ounce. Add remaining ingredients, except salad greens, and cook until snow peas and bell pepper are barely cooked (still crisp, yet tender.) Add more port if mixture becomes too dry. There should be enough sauce to lightly coat salad greens. Pour hot tenderloin over salad greens, toss gently to mix, and serve. (Serves two.)

34

Main Street Cafe Scampi

3 tablespoons olive oil
10–12 large prawns: cleaned, deveined and
    lightly floured
4 mushrooms, sliced
¼ cup tomatoes, seeded and diced
¼ cup onion, cut in thin, matchstick-size slices
½ tablespoon chopped garlic
½ teaspoon tarragon
½ teaspoon thyme
pinch of crushed red pepper
½ teaspoon chopped parsley
3 ounces white wine
4 tablespoons butter
4 tablespoons margarine
2 tablespoons lemon juice

Heat the olive oil slightly in a large sauté pan. Add prawns and lightly brown. Add mushrooms, tomatoes, onions and garlic; sauté for two minutes, tossing often. Add remaining ingredients and cook until butter and margarine are melted and all ingredients are well blended. (Serves two.)

Note: You will want to eat every drop of this delicious sauce. I suggest you serve this unusual scampi with rice and/or hot sourdough bread for effective sauce mopping.

TASTING GOLD IN
NEVADA CITY

Cirino's: busy, noisy, and no shortage of garlic.

CIRINO'S
309 Broad St., Nevada City
☎ (916) 265- 2246
Lunch and dinner every day: 11:30 a.m.–2:30 p.m. and 5 p.m.–9 p.m.
✌ Reservations strongly suggested

Robust Italian-American food; busy, family atmosphere

WALKING INTO CIRINO'S is like showing up late for dinner at your oversized Italian family's outgrown house. It's loud, it's crowded, and you may wonder if there'll be any food left by the time you find a seat.

In fact, you may not even get in without a reservation, particularly on a Wednesday or Saturday night. Cirino's serves generous portions of consistently tasty Italian-American food at prices which make it one of the most popular restaurants for families dining out in Nevada City. "We're not stuffy. We're not Victorian. If you're looking for a quiet, romantic dinner, this isn't the place," says Judy Cirino, who owns the place with husband Jerry.[1]

It's a big, casual room, with red and white checkered tablecloths and historical photos on the walls. Judy says the massive mahogany and cherry bar was built back East, then worked on San Francisco's Polk Street for some years before assuming its present location in the early 1900s.

Lunches include soups, salads, excellent hamburgers, and sandwiches, including a pair of New Yorkers: a sausage sandwich with grilled peppers and onions and a meatball sandwich with marinara (each $5.50, with soup or salad.)

1. There's another Cirino's in Downieville (located by following Highway 49 north for about an hour's scenic drive from Nevada City) which tends to be quieter, and offers outdoor dining in summer. If you plan to take sides on the local argument concerning which Cirino's serves the best food, listen to what Jerry Cirino has to say about it: "People eating in Downieville will say to me, 'You know what? This sauce is better than your sauce in Nevada City.' And I say, 'You know what? That sauce was MADE at our restaurant in Nevada City. I just brought it up here.'"

The same burgers (same prices, too!) reappear at dinnertime, alongside the pastas and other Italian-American staples. The hands-down favorite dinner item, according to Judy, is the Fettucini Alfredo. Served with soup or green salad and garlic bread, it'll set you back $8.95. Entrées like Veal Scaloppine or Piccata, New York Steak, Chicken Parmigiana or Scampi cost $10.95 to $13.95, served with soup or salad, garlic bread and a side order of pasta.

If you want something different, try a pasta special (i.e. Fettucini Alfredo with smoked trout and tomatoes) or one of the regional Italian specials like Sausage Scaloppine with Polenta and Roasted Garlic.

Cirino's Wednesday Pizza Night is a Nevada City tradition. The place usually fills up shortly after 5 and stays packed until closing, so be sure to make a reservation if you want to try this very unusual pizza. You order on a form divided in quadrants, so you can actually manage to please four squabbling family members who can't agree on sauce or toppings.

The crust is as thin and light as a cracker, and you can choose "red" (traditional tomato sauce) or "white" pizza, a wonderful olive oil and herb backdrop for your chosen toppings. Let your kids go for the red; be sure to choose the white. You can have two toppings (or pay for additional ones) chosen from a list of 12. Trust me, pick the 7/11: artichoke hearts and chopped clams. Accompanied by a glass of white wine, this is guaranteed to transport you immediately to garlic heaven. The "Four Seasons Pizza"—red or white sauce (or half and half) and two toppings on each quarter—sells for $6, $12 and $17 for small, medium and large.

PEEK AT THE PAST

The first known structure on the location now housing Cirino's was the Hotel de France, built some time before 1852 and destroyed by fire in 1856. It was rebuilt, and in 1861 was known as the Cafe National, then the Eagle Cafe, and then, by 1862, as Ferdinand Stumpf's Miners' Restaurant. A fire broke out on the site in November, 1863 which burned just about all of Nevada City except Commercial Street.

But Stumpf's Hotel and Restaurant was rebuilt and continued

to do business. An 1865 newspaper ad (in the *Nevada Transcript*) boasted that Miners Hotel and Restaurant employed "the best French cook in the state." More ad copy: "The table will be supplied with everything the market affords. English, French and German spoken at this house."

The Miners Hotel and Restaurant was sold in 1874 to Frank Eilerman, who converted the business to a saloon carrying his name. The 1898 fire map shows it as a saloon and card room with a liquor vault.

It remained a saloon for many years, sold and leased to a succession of owners. Many in Nevada City remember downing a few at (Frank) Duffy's Success before the Cirinos took over the saloon in 1983. The Cirinos have gradually converted its emphasis to food, but their Bloody Mary (served with a beer chaser) makes an appropriate beverage for toasting the location's colorful past.

John Bergman, right, and Greg Albee at Cirino's.

Cirino's Cheesecake

Crust:
> 1¼ cups graham cracker crumbs (ground in
> food processor)
> ¼ cup butter, melted

Filling:
> 1 8-ounce package cream cheese, softened
> ½ cup sugar
> 1 tablespoon freshly squeezed lemon juice
> 2 eggs
> ½ teaspoon vanilla

Topping:
> 1 cup sour cream
> 2 tablespoons sugar
> ½ teaspoon vanilla

For crust: Combine crumbs and butter, press into 8-inch pie plate.

For filling: Process cream cheese until smooth in food processor. Add other ingredients and mix until smooth. (Do not over-process.) Pour filling into prepared crust. Bake in 325-degree oven until center is just set (25-30 minutes.)

For topping: Combine ingredients. Pour topping over baked cheesecake. Return to oven and bake 10 minutes longer. Cool to room temperature. Chill thoroughly before serving.

Cirino's "Chocolate Mousse"

1 12-ounce package chocolate chips
1/2 cup boiling water
1/2 cup sugar
2 eggs
1/4 cup rum
1 1/8 cups heavy cream

Grind chocolate chips very fine in food processor. While machine is running, add boiling water and continue to process until chocolate is melted. Add sugar, eggs, and rum—mix well. With food processor running, pour in heavy cream and mix well.

Immediately pour mixture into 4-ounce dessert cups and chill well. (Serves 8 to 10.)

Cirino's Steamed Mussels Bordelaise

14 ounces fresh mussels, cleaned of beards*
olive oil
1 tablespoon minced shallots
1–3 cloves minced garlic
1 teaspoon chopped parsley
1 cup white wine
lemon slices for garnish
lemon wedges
melted butter

Heat sauté pan. Add a small amount of olive oil to barely cover the bottom of the pan. Briefly sauté the shallots, garlic, and parsley. Add mussels and wine, cover pan. Steam mussels, shaking pan occasionally, just until all the mussels have opened—about 3 to 5 minutes. Serve immediately, in accompanying broth, garnished with lemon slices. Serve with lemon wedges and melted butter for dipping mussels. (Serves two to four as an appetizer, or one person as a main course.)

*Note: Unlike clams, mussels have "beards" of fibrous material extending from inside the shell at one end. These are quickly and easily removed by pulling. Rinse mussels well after removing beards and proceed with recipe.

More'n likely the best pizza in the west.

COWBOY PIZZA
315 Spring St., Nevada City
☎ **(916) 265-2334**
Dinner only. Wednesday–Saturday: 4 p.m.–9 p.m.
Sunday: 4 p.m.–8 p.m.
✌ **Reservations necessary most nights**
Call ahead for take out

Pizza with soul

IF YOU CRAVE GREAT PIZZA and/or funky cowboy memorabilia, don't miss Cowboy Pizza. This odd marriage is the brainchild of owner Wally Hagaman, who has created a small but unique niche for himself despite cutthroat competition from pizza chains.

Don't come here looking for video games, TV, or other noisy gimmicks. Just follow your nose (they use about 2½ pounds of fresh chopped garlic A NIGHT here!) to a restored Victorian bedecked with pictures of Roy, Hoppie, Gene, and The Lone Ranger, rodeo posters, badges, and other nostalgic stuff.

Expect to wait a good 30–45 minutes after you place your order. This is real pizza—they actually build it from fresh ingredients and cook it while you wait. (If you're starving, phone ahead and they'll rustle up your pizza while you drive over.)

Munch on salad while your pizza cooks, or sip a microbrewery beer, i.e. Red Tail Ale from Hopland Brewery, for $2.12 a bottle (even the prices here are eccentric, with none of them ending in the conventional "99¢.") The scents from the kitchen will get your salivary glands worked up. Your kids can pass the time searching for Waldo in books provided for that purpose.

Cowboy's best seller is neither western nor macho. It's the Greek Vegetarian: fresh tomatoes, oregano, artichoke hearts, feta cheese from Denmark, California black olives and Gilroy garlic. It tastes great, and those who prefer meat on their pizza can get it with Canadian bacon.

Among non-vegetarians, the favorite choice is the Italian: mozzarella, provolone, cheddar and romano; Sicilian-style

45

sausage (with fennel) from Chicago, pepperoni from San Francisco; olives, fresh mushrooms, peppers, onions, and garlic on request. Another popular pizza is the Popeye: spinach, garlic, feta and pine nuts.

Wally makes his dough ("a French bread crust") fresh daily, and sells out almost nightly. He scorns mixes and space-age pizza industry components (like fake cheese called "Unique" and a non-charring meat product called "Peperoni" with one "p.") His assessment of pizza made at chains, where sauce is applied with brushes to use less of it and pepperoni arranged according to wall diagrams for uniformity: "There's no soul to it."

Wally's philosophy about food: "It should be simple. It should be hearty. It should be made with the best ingredients and the best attitude. It's important to me that it be prepared with some pride and some caring."

Most Cowboy Pizzas come in three sizes: mini, regular, and large. Prices average about $6 for a mini (a meal for one, snack for two), $12 for a regular (feeds two to three adults), and $16 for a large (feeds four-five adults). The "Children's Special Pizza" is a great idea: a mini cheese pizza for $2.59 when purchased with a regular or large pizza, so the adults can order their own exotic pizza without having to pick off all the toppings before the kids will touch it.

Ninety-seven percent of Cowboy's customers are locals. Tourists only find the place when it's recommended by somebody on the street, Wally says.

On Saturday nights, you may encounter live entertainment after 8 p.m. at Cowboy's. This could take the form of anything from belly dancing to a performance by Sourdough Slim, who sings oldtime cowboy music accompanied by his own portable cactus. Beverages are available during the shows, but they stop serving pizza at 9 p.m.

One major asset unrelated to the food: you can corral your vehicle in Cowboy's own 35-space parking lot. Anyone who's been to Nevada City on a Friday or Saturday night will appreciate the deep significance of the concept.

PEEK AT THE PAST

The present location of Cowboy Pizza dates from 1884. The 1898 fire map of Nevada City shows a dwelling on the first floor, and a saloon in the basement, with adjacent areas designated for use as a card room and for beer storage.

When the building was renovated in the late 1970s, the balustraded entry with wheelchair access was added.

Cowboy owner Wally Hagaman, home on the range.

Cowboy Pizza's Fast Pizza Crust

1 package fast-rising yeast
3 cups all purpose white flour (high-gluten flour
   is best)
1 cup hot (120–130 degrees) tap water
½ teaspoon salt

Mix the yeast with one cup of flour. Stir in the hot water and blend well. Stir in the second cup of flour and the salt. Mix until it forms a ball. Knead by hand on a floured board, adding the third cup of flour gradually until the dough is no longer sticky. (Do all kneading vigorously for about five minutes.) Dough should be smooth and "stretchy." Form into a ball.

Press dough into an 8 to 10-inch circle with your fingertips, then roll into a 15-inch circle. (To make a smaller pizza, or thinner crust, use less dough.)

**It's a stretch for Scott Hansen, eating
dinner with Susan Oldland at Cowboy Pizza.**

Cowboy Pizza's Popeye Pizza

(Proportions are approximate, according to Wally. Pizza is personal —you may have to adjust this to your taste, especially the garlic.)

1 cup tomato sauce (homemade or store-bought, see note)

1 pound to 1¼ pounds thin-sliced or grated mozzarella

1 large red onion, thinly sliced

2 10-ounce blocks frozen spinach, thawed and well-drained

½ to ¾ cup feta cheese, crumbled*

½ cup pine nuts or chopped walnuts

5 large cloves chopped garlic

Top crust (preceding recipe) with your favorite homemade or store-bought tomato sauce. Cover all but the outer ½ to ¾ inch edge of the dough. Distribute mozzarella evenly over the sauce, then add onions. Next, spread spinach evenly over the pizza and add feta. Sprinkle with nuts and fresh chopped garlic.

Bake on a cookie sheet in the middle shelf of a preheated 475-degree oven for about 15 minutes.

Note on tomato sauce: Wally says, "Tomato sauces should NEVER be boiled and only be simmered at very low heat for no more than five minutes. When possible, make the sauce cold and let it sit in the refrigerator for a day. The flavors will 'bloom' and the sauce will not be acidic. Pizza sauce should be thick, with as little water as possible."

Note on baking stones: Wally says, "If you bake breads a lot and have thought about a baking stone, but have not gotten one because of the expense, go to a ceramic supply store and buy a kiln shelf. They are cheaper and easier to use. Measure your oven shelf and buy a shelf about two inches smaller all around to allow the heat to circulate. To bake a pizza on it, just place the kiln shelf in the middle of your oven and heat as close to 500 degrees as you can get."

*Note: If you are considering increasing this amount, use caution. Some kinds of feta are overwhelmingly "goaty." There's a danger these might work better on a "Bluto" than a "Popeye."

Nevada City's most romantic spot.

FRIAR TUCK'S

111 North Pine St., Nevada City
☎ (916) 265-9093
Lunch and dinner.
Open Wednesday–Sunday at noon.
Dinner service begins at 5:30 p.m. (5 p.m.
on Sunday)
Closed Monday and Tuesday
Cocktails, wine, snacks, live music in adjacent bar
✌ Reservations strongly suggested

Tasty food; cozy, romantic setting

FRIAR TUCK'S, THE OLDEST restaurant in town under continuous ownership, is a favorite Nevada City hangout for locals and visitors alike. "Half the town's fallen in love here," according to owner Greg Cook.

It could be the candlelight, the exposed brick and big beams, the great wines, the leisurely dipped fondue, or the oversized desserts. Whatever. If romance is on your agenda, make Friar Tuck's your destination for dinner.

In two decades of operation, Cook has continually experimented to perfect his thoroughly enjoyable restaurant. "I've learned that you just try things and see what happens. My philosophy is to just gently nudge things along."

Cook's experimental tendencies mesh well with his addiction to his Macintosh, which allows him to build a fresh menu every day on his computer. This gives him and chefs Steve Lenaburg and Sandy Brill "the ultimate flexibility," varying their menu based on available fresh ingredients and fluctuating costs.

Cook finds customers, "more knowledgeable about food than they used to be, and more experimental." In addition, "People are drinking less. Since they're drinking less, they're drinking nicer stuff." New tastes and nicer wines are staples at Friar Tuck's.

Typical dinner offerings include appetizers like Soft Shelled Crab sautéed in a sweet and spicy sauce, Oysters on the Half Shell or Smoked Trout Phyllo Triangles.

Main courses (served with bread sticks and dip, soup or salad, fresh vegetables, potatoes and rice) cover a lot of ground, including choices like Steak Diablo (New York steak with green peppercorn mushroom sherry sauce), Beef Wellington, or Rack of Lamb with thyme sauce. Those who prefer surf to turf can dig into some Prawns Mazatlan (sautéed in tequila lime sauce), Hawaiian Swordfish with lemon pepper sauce or oven-roasted Salmon with cucumber, sour cream and dill sauce. Chicken and pasta dishes, including a vegetarian Pasta Radiatore with tomatoes and pesto, rounded out the menu used as a point of reference. Remember that menu offerings do change daily—from desserts to entrées. Dinner prices average $13.95–$18.95.

If you have time on your hands and some serious relaxing to do, sample the fondue that made Friar Tuck's so popular when it first opened in the early 70s. For two people, order one Alpine Cheese Fondue (a blend of Swiss Gruyère and Emmentaler, melted with wine and spices) and one of the hot oil fondues. The cheese fondue comes with cubes of French bread, apples and mushrooms for dipping. You choose what you'd like to cook in bubbling peanut oil: sirloin cubes, chicken, shrimp, lightly breaded scallops, meatballs, or some of each. (My favorites are the scallops and sirloin.) These come with assorted sauces. Your server will remind you of a critical detail of fondue technique: Remove the freshly cooked tidbit from the long cooking fork to your plate, then eat it with a regular fork so you don't burn your mouth.

This meal, accompanied by a bottle of wine, provides a sufficiently unhurried backdrop for that conversation you've been wanting to have.

Regarding wine, Friar Tuck's offers about 75 choices, including several "by the glass" specials each night. Numerous beers are offered as well.

Desserts tend to come in large portions, perfect for sharing. Typical items include Chocolate Praline Cheesecake and Chocolate Fondue accompanied by fresh fruits and pound cake squares for dipping.

With a capacity of about 150, Friar Tuck's is one of the biggest of the best in Nevada County. Whether you choose dinner or a glass of wine in the bar (which also features a less-expensive menu of no-less-tasty snacks and live music), this is the most romantic spot in town. The bar menu—featuring cheese fondue, hamburgers, steamed mussels, salads and homemade soups—is also available for lunch beginning at noon Wednesday through Sunday. Prices range from $6.95–$9.95.

But it isn't just for couples. More families are dining out these days, so Cook and his wife Rona, parents of two young children themselves, have stocked the restaurant with crayons for impatient patrons. Kids love this place, especially the fondue, and can select from an abbreviated children's menu. Cook notes that some kids, like his 4-year-old daughter, are more attracted to "adult" fare, once exposed to it. "Her favorite food is steamed clams. If we're out of clams, she'll eat mussels, but she definitely prefers clams."

PEEK AT THE PAST

The 1898 fire map of Nevada City shows the present location of Friar Tuck's as three one-story brick buildings housing separate businesses. These three, and an associated storage shed (now the Off Broad Street theatre) are thought to date from the early 1860s. The business on the corner of Pine and Commercial streets is labeled "B & S" on the fire map, which historian Ed Tyson thinks is an abbreviation for "boots and shoes." (Other possibilities we discussed include "books and stationery," or "boots and saddles.") Next in line, heading toward Broad Street, was a hardware store, and the third business sold crockery, stoves and hardware in 1898.

In 1912, the building was remodeled to its present appearance, using the services of architect J. H. Rogers. This project included construction of a second story lodge hall for use of the Nevada City Elks Club, present-day owners of the building, and the addition of large plate glass windows on street level.

Friar Tuck's Alpine Cheese Fondue

1 clove garlic
¾ cup grated Swiss Gruyère
¾ cup grated Swiss Emmentaler
⅔ cup dry white wine
1 extra shot of wine (to mix with cornstarch)
1 teaspoon cornstarch
nutmeg and pepper
1 teaspoon lemon juice
dash of kirsch
French bread, cut in cubes, for dipping
bite-sized pieces of apple and raw mushroom,
    for dipping

Rub fondue pot with garlic, discard clove. Put cheeses and wine in pot, melt slowly over stove or in microwave until blended. Mix cornstarch with a shot of wine in a cup. Stir mixture into fondue so that it is creamy blend. Add lemon juice and kirsch. Sprinkle with pepper and nutmeg. Serve over a candle warmer. Serve with French bread cubes, apple and mushroom pieces. (Serves two.)

Friar Tuck's Cashew Chicken

4 boneless chicken breasts—skin on
1 cup unsalted cashews
1 egg
⅓ cup heavy cream
fresh or dried thyme to taste
salt and pepper to taste

In a food processor, make a mousse by chopping the nuts fairly fine, then adding egg and cream and processing until smooth. Add seasonings.

Carefully lift skin away from chicken, making sure not to disconnect it completely, and stuff the cashew mousse under the skin on each piece of chicken.

Place chicken on a baking sheet, skin side up, and bake at 350 degrees for 35 minutes. (Serves four.)

Friar Tuck's Chocolate Fondue

2 cups grated chocolate or chocolate chips
½ cup half and half
splash of Triple Sec
assorted fresh fruits (i.e. strawberries, peaches,
bananas) in bite-sized pieces, for dipping
pound cake, cubed, for dipping

Slowly melt chocolate in the top of a double boiler until soft. Add half and half and liqueur, stirring, until mixture is creamy. Serve in small bowl over candle warmer. "Dip assorted items into chocolate until satisfaction has been achieved," Greg Cook advises. (Serves two or more.)

Susan Lamela enjoys Alpine
Cheese Fondue, a Friar Tuck's specialty.

Friar Tuck's Hula Pie

1 dozen Oreo cookies
¾ cup melted butter
½ to 1 gallon macadamia nut ice cream (or another flavor of your choice), depending how deep you want your pie. A gallon yields about a four-inch-deep pie.
Chocolate Sauce (recipe follows)
whipped cream for garnish

Grind up cookies finely in food processor (or crush them using a rolling pin.) Mix crumbs with melted butter. Press into an empty pie tin and freeze until firm.

Soften ice cream and shape it to fit inside the frozen cookie shell. Freeze again until firm. Top with Chocolate Sauce, cut and serve, garnished with whipped cream. (Serves six to eight.)

Friar Tuck's Chocolate Sauce

1 package chocolate chips
1 cup butter

Melt 1 package chocolate chips with 1 cup butter. Mix until smooth and pour over Hula Pie.

Friar Tuck's Lemon Pesto Salad Dressing

1 cup basil pesto
1 egg
1 tablespoon Dijon mustard
1/4 cup white wine vinegar
3/4 cup lemon juice*
1 1/2 cups olive oil

Combine first five ingredients in food processor; process one minute. With machine running, slowly add olive oil in thin stream. (Makes approximately 3 1/2 to 4 cups.) Refrigerate.

*Note: You can add more lemon juice for a thinner consistency.

Friar Tuck's Mushroom Sherry Sauce

1/4 cup margarine
1/2 cup diced onion
4 cups diced mushrooms
3/4 tablespoon crushed garlic
1/4 cup flour
1 cup water
1 tablespoon mushroom paste*
1/2 tablespoon black pepper
1 cup sherry
1/3 pound sour cream
1/4 teaspoon nutmeg

Cook margarine, onion, mushrooms, and garlic until onion is soft and ingredients are blended. Add remaining ingredients and warm gently until well mixed. Friar Tuck's serves this as a fondue sauce for cooked beef or chicken. Greg says leftover sauce will keep in the refrigerator for about two weeks.

*Note: Available in gourmet shops. If you don't have it, Greg says you can omit this ingredient and still have a tasty sauce.

Friar Tuck's Mussels in Sherry Cream Sauce

3 cloves garlic, crushed
¼ cup shallots
¼ cup butter
2 pounds fresh mussels, cleaned
dash salt and pepper
¼ cup white wine
¼ cup heavy cream
¼ cup brandy or sherry
French bread or garlic toast

Sauté garlic and shallots in butter. Add mussels, salt, pepper, wine and cream. Cover and steam until mussels open. Pour brandy or sherry in a serving bowl; add mussels and their steaming sauce. French bread or garlic toast slices make excellent devices for eating the extra sauce. (Serves two.)

Friar Tuck's Roasted Eggplant and Red Bell Pepper Soup

5 eggplants
5 red bell peppers
6 cloves garlic
olive oil
1 quart milk
1 quart half and half
salt and white pepper to taste

Peel eggplants and chop. Seed bell peppers and cut each into several pieces. Peel garlic. Coat everything with olive oil and spread on baking sheet. Roast in a 350-degree oven until vegetables are soft. Purée in food processor until smooth. Add milk, half and half and seasonings. (Serves six.)

Friar Tuck's Shellfish Delight

¼ cube butter
½ teaspoon minced garlic
½ teaspoon crushed shallots
4 jumbo prawns
4 ounces scallops
6 ounces lobster tail, cut into pieces
¼ cup chopped parsley
½ cup sliced mushrooms
¼ cup white wine
¼ heavy cream

Melt butter into sauté pan, add garlic and shallots and sauté briefly. Add shellfish and sauté until nearly done. Add mushrooms and parsley, sauté until done. Add white wine and reduce; add heavy cream, thicken, and serve. (Serves two.)

Steven Slaser and Melonie Sykes at Friar Tuck's.

MICHAEL'S GARDEN RESTAURANT

216 Main Street, Nevada City
☎ (916) 265- 6660
Lunch: Tuesday–Saturday 11:30 a.m.–2:30 a.m.
(April through December)
Dinner: Monday–Saturday, 5:30 p.m.–9 p.m.
✌ Reservations suggested, especially on weekends

Very tasty food, including "custom" meals

STEPPING INTO THIS FORMER Victorian home could remind you of visiting Great Aunt Lucy for tea, but there's nothing staid about the food here. For starters, you can order at Michael's Garden without consulting a menu.

You just tell chef/owner Michael Daley your parameters in terms of food (for example, you prefer a dinner focused on seafood or a low-calorie meal) and price ($18 to $100 per person). He'll mastermind a custom meal especially for you and your party, using a process he refers to as "Michael's Menu." Your custom meal is served family-style, with everyone eating the same thing, so you need to make sure your group contains like-minded diners. (It's best to make "Michael's Menu" arrangements in advance by phone, especially if you're showing up on a crowded Saturday night.)

"A lot of people—because they lead a structured life—like Michael's Menu because it offers the luxury of not having to make another decision. They don't even have to read the menu," Michael explains. "People just come in and have faith and allow us to present fresh what we find in the market right now."

This isn't exactly blind faith. Michael has his share of devotees who swear his is the best restaurant in Nevada City. His food preparation is inventive, featuring high quality ingredients.

For first-timers, timid traditionalists, or others who just like ordering from a menu, thank you very much, there's plenty to choose from at Michael's Garden. Entrées include prawns, scallops, calamari, "Seasonal Seafood Combination," New York steak, filet mignon, chicken breast, duck, vegetables, or pasta.

61

Most are offered in two or more styles, i.e. the prawns can be ordered sautéed in garlic butter, broiled with teriyaki sauce, or sautéed with hot and spicy sauce. Dinner prices range from $8.95 –$14.95, including soup and salad, rice, and two vegetables.

A Michael's Garden signature item served with all entrées is carrot purée. I know, I know. It sounds like something your mother unsuccessfully tried to force you to eat, but trust me. It's unbelievable that anything called carrot purée—consisting of nothing but steamed carrots puréed with a tiny bit of heavy cream—can taste this good.

In warm weather, you can eat in the garden out back, surrounded by Japanese maples and bamboo. In cooler weather, Michael's Garden expands into several rooms of the quaint Victorian to accommodate a crowd.

Lunch, served April through December, includes assorted salads, soups, pastas and sandwiches, priced from $3–$10.

Michael was a waiter here for five years before he bought the place in 1985, so he knows the business from a couple of angles. His love for his work is obvious in the meals he prepares, and Michael likes talking about food almost as much as other people like eating his cooking.

PEEK AT THE PAST

Originally built as a one-story home in 1870, the building now housing Michael's Garden Restaurant was remodeled and enlarged into the present two-story building about 1890. The ornamental Victorian bay windows facing Main Street had been added by 1898 and those on the side of the building were in place by 1912.

On March 6, 1888, Oscar Maltman deeded the property to Emma Maltman, who sold it for $10 in 1905 to J. V. Snyder. It was part of his estate in 1923. Other owners over the years have included Steve and Cathy Cooke, Stan Miller, and Otto and Monica Fischer.

The building has been used for residential purposes most of its life, but was converted to commercial use sometime in the late 1960s. At one time, The Herb Shop (now at 107 North Pine, Nevada City) was located in part of the downstairs area. A series of restaurants preceded Michael's Garden, which opened in 1984.

Michael's Garden Aïoli Sauce

6 egg yolks
6 teaspoons fresh puréed garlic
3 teaspoons lemon juice
2 teaspoons mustard
½ teaspoon salt
½ teaspoon white pepper
3 cups olive oil

Put all ingredients but olive oil in the food processor. Start motor and drizzle in olive oil with motor running until you have a fine garlic mayonnaise. Makes about 3½ cups. Leftovers can be stored in the refrigerator for several days. Michael says this aïoli is "perfect for topping fish or dipping vegetables."

Wayne and Kathie McIntosh get their fill from waitress Jennifer Knapp at Michael's Garden Restaurant.

Michael's Garden Blue Cheese Salad Dressing

1 quart mayonnaise
1½ cups blue cheese, crumbled
¾ cup buttermilk
3 shots Tabasco sauce (a shot equals a quick
    shake of the bottle)
¼ tablespoon garlic purée
¼ tablespoon Worchestershire sauce
¼ teaspoon white pepper
¼ teaspoon salt.

Mix gently, allowing some of the blue cheese crumbles to stay in chunks (rather than making a totally smooth purée.) Adjust seasonings to taste. Refrigerate. Keeps up to one week.

Michael's Garden Filo Prawns

For each serving:
    one large prawn
    one sheet of filo pastry (available frozen in
        supermarkets)
    butter
    slice of Monterey Jack cheese
        (approximately 2″ × 1″ × ⅛″)
    pinch of dried basil
    dash of garlic powder
    dash of pepper

Preheat oven to 350 degrees. Peel and devein the prawn. Butter a sheet of filo pastry and fold it in half. Put the cheese slice on filo and the prawn on top of it. Rub the basil through your fingers and sprinkle on top of prawn. Add garlic powder and pepper. Roll the filo into what Michael calls, "a shape you're comfortable with" to make a container, remembering that the cheese is going to melt. Bake 7–10 minutes. When the outside is browned and the cheese is melted, the prawn will be cooked.

Michael's Garden Lemon Cheesecake

1 pound cottage cheese
2 pounds cream cheese
1½ cups sugar
4 eggs
1 teaspoon vanilla
⅓ cup cornstarch
2 to 2½ tablespoons lemon juice
1 teaspoon vanilla
½ cup melted margarine
1 pint sour cream
about 1 teaspoon butter for pan
ground nuts or graham crackers for dusting
    inside of pan (optional)
fresh or puréed raspberries for garnish

Blend all ingredients except butter, nuts, graham crackers and raspberries in food processor until smooth. Taste and adjust lemon juice if necessary. Butter a spring-form pan, dust inside with crushed nuts or graham cracker crumbs if you like. Pour batter into pan and bake at 325 degrees for one hour. Check firmness, and if loose, bake 10 minutes more. If texture is stable, remove from oven and let cool. Refrigerate. Serve with fresh or puréed raspberries. (Serves about 16.)

Michael's Garden Persimmon Pudding Cake

3 tablespoons butter
1½ cups sugar
5 teaspoons vanilla
1½ cups seedless raisins
1 teaspoon ground cloves
2 eggs
1½ cups puréed persimmon pulp
¼ cup milk or cream
1½ cups chopped walnuts or other nuts
2¼ cups sifted flour
1½ teaspoons baking soda
1 teaspoon salt
1½ teaspoons cinnamon
whipped cream for garnish

Mix all dry ingredients. Combine wet ingredients separately, then blend with dry ingredients. Grease and flour a large pan that you can put on a trivet inside a larger steaming pot. Fill about ⅗ full and cover with aluminum foil secured with rubber bands or ties. Steam for 1½ hours. Check to see if it needs more cooking. Cake is done when toothpick inserted in the center comes out clean. When done, let cool. Serve with whipped cream. (Serves about 12.)

Michael's Garden
Simple No-Cook Teriyaki Sauce

1¼ cups soy sauce
1¼ cups water
¼ pound brown sugar
¾ tablespoon minced fresh ginger
¼ bunch chopped green onion
¼ tablespoon puréed garlic
¼ tablespoon black pepper

Mix all ingredients well. Adjust seasonings to taste. Makes about a quart. "You can put this in the refrigerator for a month, and it'll only get better," Michael says. He doesn't like to marinate food "because it changes the texture." He likes to pour some of this sauce into an individual-size baking dish, then bake chicken in it for chicken teriyaki. Another suggestion from Michael: "Try baking oyster mushrooms in teriyaki sauce for 8–10 minutes at 350 degrees. They're just outrageous." Sometimes, he reduces the sauce (by boiling, uncovered) to a syrup, using it as a glaze, "for a bigger taste."

Nevada City's garden of delights—Michael's Garden Restaurant.

Well worth the trip off the beaten track.

THE NORTHRIDGE INN
773 Nevada Street, Nevada City
☎ (916) 265-2206
Lunch and dinner
Sunday–Thursday, 11:30 a.m.–9 p.m.;
Friday and Saturday, 11:30 a.m.–10 p.m.

Burgers, shakes, brews and nostalgia

THE NORTHRIDGE INN IS A two-minute drive (and decently challenging walk) from Nevada City, in a location unlikely to be discovered by tourists. (To get there from downtown, head down Broad Street, cross the freeway and take a sharp left. You'll cross Deer Creek on a little bridge, then head up Nevada Street's extremely steep hill. Various intersections may tempt you, but STAY on winding Nevada Street at all costs. If it happens to be autumn, you'll see some maple trees which will make you think you're in Vermont. And after about a mile, whether it's autumn or not, you'll see The Northridge on your right. If you come to Highway 20/49, you've gone too far.)

Inside, it's knotty pine, it's cozy, and there's sawdust on the floor (not a souvenir of recent repairs, but purposely added for "personality" according to owner Jordan Klempner.) The Northridge qualifies as the most casual spot in town, a great place to kick back and take a binge down memory lane to the pre-cholesterol era.

If you've walked from downtown (a course of action not recommended for anyone remembering a recent cardiac arrest, but good for assuaging the guilt you may soon feel after wrecking your diet) you'll certainly be ready for a beer or one of The Northridge's yummy old-fashioned (i.e. real) milkshakes or malts. These nostalgia-invoking concoctions come in traditional vanilla, chocolate and strawberry, served in 50s soda fountain glasses with extra portions alongside in rime-covered stainless

69

steel containers. (Yes, Virginia, they also have Hot Fudge Sundaes here.)

Beer nuts will know they've come to the right place, with The Northridge's awe-inspiring selection of more than 60 varieties. Choose between 15 types of draft beer, including the excellent local product—Nevada City Brew.

For purists, the obvious choice to accompany one's beer or shake is a burger, in this case the appropriately-named "The Northridge Inn 9-Napkin Burger." It's one-third pound of beef served with lettuce, tomato, onion and thousand island dressing, garnished with tortilla chips and salsa for under $5. Add 85 cents for some very serious French fries, complete with skins.

Other popular items include Philly Cheese Steak and Chicken Sonora sandwiches and homemade soups. Dieters may prefer one of the five kinds of salad (i.e. the BBQ Chicken Salad featuring chunks of barbequed chicken, lettuce, mushrooms, onions, tomatoes and mozzarella.) And vegetarians will be relieved to find Tabbouli and Falafel (both served with sesame tahini dressing and pita), Tofu Twin Hot Dogs (I admit I haven't gotten up the nerve to try these) and Vegi Burgers.

The most expensive item on the menu is $7.50 (for a Double Burger with Bacon and Cheese), which makes this one of the most reasonable places to chow in Nevada City. For this reason, it can be crowded and noisy. "Kids are welcome at all times. We're trying to make it one of the few places you can go and bring your kids and have a good time," says Jordan, who owns The Northridge with partner Barbara Paul.

A new kids' menu for those 10 or under features four meals untainted by repulsive green things, each served with a soft drink, for $2.95.

Jordan, who has a degree in business administration, owned a restaurant in Los Angeles for 15 years before taking over The Northridge in 1990. A closet musician, he added live music Thursday, Friday (bluegrass) and Saturday nights, beginning around 7:30 p.m.

PEEK AT THE PAST

According to George Nelson, who retired after working for Nevada City for 30 years and knows a great deal about local buildings, this structure is "not that old." Nelson said it was built about 1946 by Andy Rogers as a store and gas station.

Some time in the 1950s, Nelson said, the place was taken over by a mechanic named Charles Mendonca and his wife. Mr. Mendonca enlarged the building to include a place for repairing autos and ran it until the 1960s.

By the 1970s, the place was functioning as a cafe, and called The Northridge. In 1977, Henry Enns bought it from Peggy Peterson, and he was running the cafe when Dale Teubert bought it in 1982.

Teubert, who had earlier won lots of fans with his Hardrock Saloon in Grass Valley (now Main Street Cafe), also worked his magic at The Northridge, redoing the acrylic bar and adding knotty pine booths and tables. Then he stocked the place with an impressive array of imported beers. His wife Dixie was responsible for the kitchen, where she actually invented The 9-Napkin Hamburger, Dale noted.

And he explained that The Northridge wasn't always off the beaten track. "Old Highway 20 came right up Nevada Street," he explained. (That was before the Highway 49/20 freeway was completed in the mid-1960s.) And even earlier, stagecoaches heading for the town of Washington would pass right by the present location of The Northridge, according to historian Ed Tyson.

The Northridge Inn Chicken Sonora

For each serving:

- 1 boneless, skinless chicken breast
- 1 teaspoon vegetable oil (if frying the chicken)
- 3 tablespoons salsa (approximately)
- 1 slice Cheddar cheese
- 1 hamburger bun
- 4 slices tomato
- 1 large lettuce leaf
- 1 teaspoon mayonnaise

Grill the chicken breast or fry it in 1 teaspoon of oil. After one side is cooked, turn the chicken and spoon salsa on the cooked side, then top with cheese. The cheese melts while the chicken finishes cooking. (To test for doneness, pierce the thickest part of the chicken breast with a fork or knife. If the juice is clear, the chicken is done.) When cooked, place on a hamburger bun with mayonnaise, lettuce and tomato and serve.

The Northridge Inn's kick back cuisine enjoyed by Candace Hansen and owner Jordan Klempner.

The Northridge Inn Philly Cheese Steak

For each serving:
   2 teaspoons vegetable oil
   5 ounces *thinly* sliced ribeye steak
   ¼ onion, sliced
   2 mushrooms, sliced
   ¼ green bell pepper, sliced
   salt and pepper to taste
   2 slices mozzarella
   hot, toasted 8-inch bun or French roll

Heat oil in large frying pan. Add meat and vegetables and cook together, lightly salting and peppering. When everything is nearly cooked, melt mozzarella on top. Place cooked ingredients on bun or French roll and serve.

Ribeye steak is "the only meat to use" for this sandwich, Jordan insists, and it must be *thinly* sliced. "Underline thinly, that's the key," according to Jordan. "I learned this 30 years ago from a guy from Philadelphia whose restaurant is still going," he notes.

Serious French fries crowd a Philly Cheese
Steak at the Northridge Inn.

PETER SELAYA'S

320 Broad Street, Nevada City
☎ **(916) 265-5697**
Dinner (If you want a picnic lunch, see *Selaya's*
Gourmet Food To Go **on page 92)**
Tuesday–Thursday, 6 p.m.–9 p.m.;
Friday, 6 p.m.–9:30 p.m.;
Saturday 5:30 p.m.–9:30 p.m.;
Sunday 5 p.m.–9 p.m.
✌ **Reservations strongly suggested**

Fabulous, innovative food;
Victorian setting

THIS IS NEVADA COUNTY'S MOST sophisticated restaurant—the place to take know-it-alls or someone you're trying to impress. It's one of those seldom-found spots where you can safely expect one of the best meals of your life every time you walk through the door, accompanied by a comfortable, unpretentious ambiance. Everything at Selaya's is as beautiful, fresh and surprising as the floral arrangements decorating the women's bathroom.

Don't be misled by the warm, friendly demeanor of owners Peter Selaya and his wife, Donna Taggart. These people are totally uncompromising. "It's just important to us to have the best," he says, with typical directness. That means organic produce and poultry and "chemical-free beef when we can get it." It means making all their own breads and pastas.

No matter how jaded your palate, you'll savor appetizers like Barbecued Oysters, Smoked Salmon Carpaccio and Blue Walnut Mushrooms (stuffed with roasted walnuts and blue cheese.) Salads, offered a la carte, include Smoked Trout Salad (fresh lettuces with smoked trout, capers, pine nuts and olives) and Spinach Salad with feta cheese, mushrooms, red onion and garlic croutons, served with a sun-dried tomato vinaigrette. (No bacon or hard-boiled eggs!)

If you live by the Italian credo: "A meal without pasta is like a day without sunshine," don't leave without sampling Peter's melt-in-your-mouth pasta dishes. Choose from Gnocci Parisienne made with gorgonzola; Fettucine made with three cheeses and topped with fresh tomato sauce; or the Market Ravioli of the day. A typical Selaya's ravioli contains smoked fresh mozzarella, romano, spinach, and pine nuts, served in a surprising roasted red pepper sauce. Additional pasta specials (such as saffron tagliarini with sun-dried tomatoes, smoked chicken and asparagus) are frequently offered. Pasta dishes are served with fresh vegetables, Selaya's irresistible homemade baguettes, and butter.

Dinner entrées cover a lot of ground: fish, fowl, meat and vegetarian, all served with vegetables, rice or potatoes, baguettes and butter. Vegetarians tired of lame-brained fare some restaurants push at them will enjoy "The Gourmet Vegetarian": seasonal vegetables baked in pastry with cheese and garlic butter, served with cashew-stuffed mushrooms. Other entrées include Fresh Salmon (grilled with mustard caper aïoli), Scallops Rockefeller (Pernod gives this dish tangy depth), Tornedos Béarnaise wrapped in prosciutto, Roast Duck (roasted with whole garlic and Zinfandel sauce) and an ever-changing list of tempting specials.

Speaking of temptation, they take desserts seriously here. As my grandmother frequently advised at her dinner table, "Don't hold back." The homemade cheesecakes, tortes, tarts and ice cream are guaranteed to blow your mind and your diet.

If you stubbornly insist on sticking to a special diet, come hollandaise or high water, Peter will cook anything to suit your restrictions. "We're happy to work with you, especially if you give me a little time. We want people to have a good time. I like it when people want different things."

Average prices per person are: appetizers, $7; salads, $5; pasta dishes, $10; dinners, $15.

One other detail: No smoking is permitted at Selaya's.

PEEK AT THE PAST

Sam Rogers built and operated a bakery here in the early 1850s, and it burned in 1856. He sold to Alexander Gault, a native of Ireland, who opened a bakery at the present location of Selaya's circa 1866. The present structure is thought to have been erected in approximately 1880. An item in the *Nevada County Mining Review*, published about 1896, says, "Mr. Gault has raised a large family, and is an enterprising, public-spirited citizen. His bakery on Broad Street is known to all, and enjoys a large share of public patronage."

The 1898 fire map for Nevada City shows the front of the building as a dwelling, with the rear part used as a bakery, as designated by fire-preventive brick and sand under the roof. In back of the bakery was an area used to store fuel for the huge oven, which reportedly burned a cord of wood a day baking bread for miners. (The walled-over oven exists behind Selaya's present kitchen.)

Gault sold the business in 1903 and two other owners operated the bakery before it was transferred to Karl Kopp in 1922. Kopp and his son Lou ran the bakery for 20 years; then Lou continued operating the business with his son, Norman, adding a fountain and lunch counter. That use persisted until the 1970s, when the building was remodeled into a restaurant. To many long-time residents, the location is still referred to as "Kopps' Bakery."

Peter Selaya's Ahi with Black Bean Salsa

2 ahi steaks, approximately 6–7 ounces each
3 tablespoons olive oil
1 clove garlic, chopped
1/8 teaspoon black pepper
juice of 1 lime
Black Bean Salsa (recipe follows)

Marinate ahi in remaining ingredients, mixed, for 15–20 minutes. Grill or sauté until done. (Serves two.) Serve each portion with approximately 1/4 cup Black Bean Salsa.

Peter Selaya's Black Bean Salsa

2 cups black beans, cooked
1 fresh jalapeño, diced*
1/4 cup red bell pepper, diced
3 or 4 green onions, sliced
1 clove garlic, crushed
1/4 cup tomato, diced
1/4 cup yellow bell pepper, diced
3 tablespoons olive oil
2 limes: juice and zest
salt and pepper to taste
2 tablespoons chopped cilantro

Mix all ingredients and let marinate for one to two hours before serving.

In addition to ahi, this salsa is good on salmon, bass or chicken. And Peter says leftover salsa is "great the next day over rice."

Note: This may be a little hot. To cool it down, remove seeds or use less of the meat.

Peter Selaya's Basic Tart Dough

½ cup sugar
4½ cups all purpose flour
3 egg yolks
¾ pound butter, cold
½ cup whipping cream

Place sugar, flour and butter into food processor and blend until crumbly. Add egg yolks and whipping cream and blend until absorbed. Remove and refrigerate approximately one hour before using. Makes enough crust for one 12-inch tart and lattice top. (Tart recipes follow.)

Owner Donna Taggart lists Selaya's nightly specials.

Peter Selaya's Blueberry Mascarpone Tart

1 pound mascarpone*
2 baskets fresh blueberries†
1 cup sugar
1 lemon, juiced
Basic Tart Dough (see recipe)

Roll out dough and place into 12-inch tart pan. Make sure there are no cracks in bottom or sides. Spread mascarpone over bottom. Set aside.

Place blueberries in saucepan with sugar and lemon juice. Cook until liquid has dissolved down to half. Let cool approximately 30 minutes. Pour over tart.

If you have extra dough, you can make a lattice on top for decoration. (None is needed.)

Place foil on bottom of oven to catch any boilovers. Bake at 350 degrees for one to one and a half hours until crust is dark brown (not burnt.) (Serves 12 to 14.)

* *Note:* If you live in Western Nevada County, one place you can find this Italian cream cheese is at Peter's own Gourmet Food To Go (110 York St., Nevada City.) If can't get your hands on any mascarpone, you can substitute cream cheese, thinned with a little whipping cream, with a tiny bit of lemon juice added for tanginess.

† *Note:* Blackberries or raspberries are good substitutes for blueberries.

Peter Selaya's Cappucino Cheesecake

Graham cracker crust
2 pounds cream cheese
5 eggs
¾ cup sugar
¾ cup espresso (or other strong, brewed coffee
 like French roast)
2½ cups sour cream
3 ounces melted chocolate
¼ cup sugar

Butter a 9½- to 10-inch spring-form pan. Press crust into bottom of pan.

Combine cream cheese, eggs, ¾ cup sugar, and espresso in mixer and blend until creamy. Pour into pan. Bake 35 minutes at 350 degrees. Remove from oven and cool 30 minutes.

Mix sour cream, chocolate and ¼ cup sugar.

Gently pour over cheesecake and bake for 5–7 minutes at 350 degrees. Remove and let cool for one hour, then refrigerate at least five hours before serving. (Serves 12 to 14.)

Peter Selaya's Carmel Espresso Walnut Tart

2 ½ cups sugar

1 ½ cups whipping cream

1 cup strong espresso* or other strong, brewed
   coffee like French roast

2 ounces butter

1 teaspoon vanilla

3 eggs

about 2½ to 3 cups walnuts (or pecans, if you
   prefer)

Basic Tart Dough (see recipe)

Roll dough out and place into 12-inch tart pan. Make sure there are no cracks in bottom or sides. Set aside.

Caramelize 2½ cups sugar. When sugar is light amber, add whipping cream. Cook at low temperature until sugar is dissolved. (Be careful—this has a tendency to boil over.) When sugar has dissolved and mixture is thick, remove from heat. Add espresso, butter, vanilla, and eggs. Mix until blended.

Spread enough walnuts on tart shell to cover it. Pour caramel over nuts. Bake in 350-degree over for one hour to an hour and 15 minutes until crust is dark (not burnt.)† (Serves 12 to 14.)

*_Note:_ Espresso may be left out. Increase whipping cream if deleting espresso.

†_Note:_ Peter bakes tarts longer than most people, he says, which "gets the fat out and leaves a nice nutty flavor."

Peter Selaya's Chocolate Torte

**14 ounces hazelnuts or almonds
2 tablespoons flour
2 tablespoons cocoa powder
6 ounces bitter chocolate
2 ounces butter
9 eggs, separated
1 cup sugar
1 cup apricot jam
Chocolate Sauce (recipe follows)**

Place nuts, flour, and cocoa powder in food processor and blend until finely chopped. Set aside.

Place bitter chocolate and butter in top of double boiler and melt. When melted, cool—set aside.

Whip egg yolks with ½ cup sugar. Whip until thick and linen-colored. Set aside.

Whip egg whites until stiff. Slowly add ½ cup sugar and whip until thick and creamy.

Fold ⅓ egg whites into egg yolks, then add ½ the nut mixture. Repeat. Add in final ⅓ egg whites, then fold in melted chocolate.

Pour into buttered and lined (with a piece of parchment buttered on both sides) spring-form pan. Bake at 350 degrees for approximately 40 minutes, or until a toothpick comes out clean.

Remove from oven and let cool approximately one hour. Remove outer ring. Glaze with melted apricot jam.

Serve with Chocolate Sauce. (Serves 10 to 12.)

Peter Selaya's Chocolate Sauce

**6 ounces bitter chocolate
8 ounces whipping cream
1 ounce cognac**

Melt all ingredients in the top of a double boiler and blend. Serve warm over Chocolate Torte. (Makes enough sauce for one torte.)

Peter Selaya's Halibut with Crab Stuffing/Cucumber Sauce

2 servings halibut, 6–7 ounces each
4 ounces fresh crab
1 cucumber—peeled, seeded, sliced
1 tablespoon butter for cooking
salt and white pepper to taste
2 tablespoons flour for dredging
¾ cup whipping cream
¼ cup white wine
juice of 1 lemon
1 clove garlic, crushed
1 tablespoon fresh parsley, chopped
1 tablespoon tomato, diced

Make pocket in each filet with sharp knife. Stuff each with 2 ounces crab meat. Dredge in flour. Sauté in hot butter until golden on one side, turn over. Add garlic, cucumbers, salt and pepper, wine, lemon juice, cream. Cover pan and steam until fish is cooked, approximately 4–5 minutes.

Remove fish from pan. Continue cooking sauce until thick. Add parsley and pour sauce over fish. Sprinkle diced tomatoes over sauce and serve at once. (Serves two.)

Donna Taggart and Peter Selaya have created the county's most polished gem.

Peter Selaya's Lemon Blackberry Terrine

5 eggs
¾ cup sugar
6 cups (3 pints or 1½ quarts) whipping cream
4 lemons, zest and juice
3 cups *frozen* blackberries*
Blackberry Sauce (recipe follows)
additional whipped cream for decoration

Cook eggs, sugar, and 3 cups whipping cream (unwhipped) in top of double boiler until it starts to get thick. Add lemon zest and juice, cook until thick. Remove custard from heat and cool.

Whip the remaining 3 cups of cream. Fold whipped cream into lemon custard. Fold in blackberries. Pour mixture into loaf mold lined with plastic wrap. Cover and freeze overnight.

Remove from mold onto serving platter. Remove plastic wrap and slice for serving.

Serve with Blackberry Sauce and dollops or stars made out of whipped cream, if desired. (About 10 servings.)

**Note:* Do not thaw or dessert will be streaked with blackberry juice.

Peter Selaya's Blackberry Sauce

2 cups blackberries
¼ to ½ cup sugar
juice of 1 lemon

Place berries in saucepan, add lemon juice and sugar* to taste. Boil slowly to release the juice, then strain the sauce to remove seeds. Do not force through your sieve or sauce will be cloudy.

**Note:* Peter says the sugar acts as a preservative in this sauce. If you add ½ cup, the sauce will keep about 3 weeks, refrigerated. If you add less, the sauce won't stay fresh as long.

Peter Selaya's Pasta with Smoked Chicken

2 servings pasta (fettucini, tagliarini, etc)
   cooked al dente
1 tablespoon butter for cooking
2 cloves garlic, chopped
1/4 cup pine nuts, toasted
1 1/2 cups asparagus, sliced
1/4 cup sun-dried tomatoes, sliced
4–5 ounces smoked chicken, sliced
1 1/2 cups whipping cream
salt and white pepper to taste
1/4 to 1/2 cup fresh grated Romano

Heat butter in sauté pan, add garlic and asparagus. Sauté until tender. Add sun-dried tomatoes, pine nuts, smoked chicken, pasta, whipping cream, salt and pepper to taste.

Cook until cream has thickened into sauce. Pour onto plates. Sprinkle Romano on top and serve immediately. (Serves two.)

Peter Selaya's Roasted Red Pepper Soup

7–8 red bell peppers
2 large yellow onions,
   sliced
2 bulbs garlic
1 tablespoon olive oil
4 stalks celery, sliced
salt and white pepper to
   taste
1½ tablespoons fresh
   thyme or fresh
   oregano*

¼ cup sherry
pinch cayenne pepper
3–4 quarts strong
   chicken stock
sour cream, yellow bell
   pepper or sliced
   green onion for
   garnish
French bread as
   accompaniment

Light the gas burner on your stove† and roast bell peppers one at a time over the open flame, using tongs to rotate and taking care not to burn yourself. Skin will become blackened. Place in paper bag to steam. When cool, peel off skin under cool running water and remove seeds. Purée in food processor—set aside.

Pour a little olive oil over garlic bulbs and roast in oven until light brown and bubbly. Remove and let cool. Squeeze garlic out and set aside.

Sauté onions and celery in olive oil until lightly caramelized. Add to stock and slightly boil for about 30 minutes. Add salt and pepper, garlic, thyme. Cook 15 minutes, strain, and put stock back on the stove. Purée onion mixture and add back to stock with red peppers. Bring to a light boil. Be careful not to burn—it might stick. Add sherry and cayenne. Turn off heat and serve.

Serve garnished with a dab of sour cream and diced yellow pepper (either roasted, when you roast the red ones, or left crunchy for a contrasting texture) or sliced green onions. Serve with French bread. (Serves six for dinner, with leftovers.)

*Note: Peter says leave this out if you don't have any fresh herbs. He cautions against substituting dried herbs because "they always taste like straw."

†Note: If you have an electric stove, roast the peppers by putting them in a 400-degree oven until the skin blisters and turns brown—about 20–30 minutes. Then proceed as directed.

Chef/owner Peter Selaya bakes tarts longer for nutty flavor.

Peter Selaya's Salmon Oriental

2 pieces salmon filet, approximately 6–7 ounces
    each
$\frac{1}{2}$ cup sake
$\frac{1}{8}$ cup soy sauce
1 tablespoon fresh ginger, grated
4 tablespoons sesame oil
1 clove garlic, crushed
fresh chive spears (for garnish)

Combine sake, soy sauce, ginger and 2 tablespoons of the sesame oil. Marinate salmon steaks in the mixture for approximately 15–20 minutes.

Heat sauté pan. Add 2 tablespoons sesame oil. Brown fish on one side, turn over, add garlic. Cook for a few minutes, add marinade to pan and cover to steam for approximately 3–4 minutes.

When fish is done, remove from pan. Reduce sauce and pour over salmon steaks. Garnish with fresh chive spears. (Serves two.)

Peter Selaya's Smoked Salmon Carpaccio

2–3 ounces smoked salmon, sliced
1 lemon, juiced
$\frac{1}{4}$ cup extra virgin olive oil
fresh cracked pepper to taste
capers and sliced red onion for garnish
baguette

Place olive oil, lemon juice and pepper in plate or shallow bowl. Dredge salmon in olive oil mixture. Place on serving plate.

Garnish with capers and sliced red onion. Serve with sliced baguette. (Serves two.)

Peter Selaya's Smoked Trout Salad

4 cups (approximately) mixed lettuces,
   washed and torn in bite-sized pieces
3–4 ounces smoked trout, broken into small
   pieces
4 slices red onion
2 tablespoons capers
12 pitted black olives
4 tablespoons pine nuts, toasted
Balsamic Dressing (recipe follows)
Ripe cherry or sliced tomatoes and Belgian
   endive for garnish

Place lettuce in bowl. Add smoked trout, red onion, capers, olives and pine nuts. Toss lightly to mix. Add just enough dressing to coat lettuce.

Place on serving plates. Garnish with tomatoes and Belgian endive. (Serves two.)

Peter Selaya's Balsamic Dressing

1 tablespoon Dijon mustard
1 clove garlic, crushed
2 tablespoons shallots, chopped fine
1 tablespoon parsley, chopped
salt and pepper
1/3 cup balsamic vinegar
2/3 cup extra virgin olive oil*
1/3 cup expeller-pressed safflower oil

Mix mustard, garlic, shallots, parsley, salt, pepper, balsamic vinegar in bowl. Slowly add the oils while mixing with a whisk.

Leftover dressing will keep, refrigerated, about two weeks.

*Note: If olive oil is too strongly flavored, you want to use 1/2 cup olive oil and 1/2 cup safflower oil, according to Peter.

Peter Selaya's Stuffed Squash Blossoms

6 large squash blossoms (i.e. pumpkin)
6 tablespoons goat cheese (approximately)*
flour
Beer Batter (recipe follows)
oil for frying

Stuff blossoms with goat cheese, about one tablespoon of cheese per blossom. Toss in flour (to make the Beer Batter stick better), then dip in Beer Batter. Fry in hot oil until golden brown. Drain on paper and serve. (Serves two.)

*Note: Different types of cheeses may be used. Peter says herbed cream cheese mixtures are good.

Peter Selaya's Beer Batter

¾ cup flour
1 teaspoon baking powder
pinch of salt
1 egg
approximately 6 ounces lager beer
3 tablespoons buttermilk

Combine all ingredients in bowl and mix. Batter should be thick enough to coat blossoms. Keep refrigerated until use.

SELAYA'S GOURMET FOOD TO GO

110 York St., Nevada City
☎ (916) 265-0558
Monday–Friday, 11 a.m. to 6 p.m.

Picnic chic quick

WHEN IT'S TOO HOT TO COOK, or you need a picnic lunch in a rush, visit this micro-deli, located around the corner from Peter Selaya's fine restaurant.

The food is a different bag of tricks from what you find in the restaurant, but you'll notice the same top quality ingredients and interesting combinations. Here the emphasis is on sandwiches, salads, chicken dishes, baguettes, pizza, and desserts.

This is the place to find a Smoked Trout Sandwich merging that delicacy with cream cheese, lettuce, tomato, onion, and capers, for $5.35. Other sandwiches built around turkey, London broil, salami, ham, or veggies can be ordered as well, for under $5 apiece. Light eaters can get half-sandwich portions.

Soups and salads vary daily. Typical offerings include pasta salad or Waldorf Salad with Gruyère cheese, about $3.25 a half-pound. Daily hot items such as Potato Leek Soup or Black Bean Chili come in small, medium, or large portions for $1.50–$4.

Or you can have one of Peter's Pizzas for $2.50.

Don't consider leaving without dessert, especially if you're a chocoholic. Here's your chance to sample an R-rated adult dessert like Chocolate Mousse Torte or Chocolate Raspberry Cake in the privacy of your own home, for about $1.50 per slice.

TASTING GOLD IN TRUCKEE

No matter how cold it is outside, it's cozy at OB's.

OB'S PUB AND RESTAURANT

Commercial Row, Truckee

☎ **(916) 587-4164**

Lunch from 11:30 a.m.;

Dinner nightly from 5:30 p.m.,

Weekend brunch 9 a.m.–2 p.m.

✌ **Reservations not accepted**

Something for everyone

O N YOUR FIRST VISIT to OB's, you'll notice that the place offers three distinct eating areas (not counting an upstairs banquet room.) You can go for anything from the romantic high-backed dark wood booths to the cozy bustle of the bar.

All the rooms are comfortable, decorated with old photos, funky antique light fixtures and memorabilia such as the long-handled tools used to get things in and out of the oven back when part of OB's was a bakery.

The current incarnation, as restaurant, began in 1970 as an Irish pub in the present bar. Over time, OB's has expanded to become the biggest restaurant in Truckee, but it never lost the friendly, pubby feeling. Dick Howell, who started at OB's as a waiter in 1972, now owns the place with Mike Linnett.

Comparing the current operation with those early days, Howell says, "We've changed a lot of things," such as diversifying from the original ribs, steak and tempura menu into a plentiful array of salads, pastas, seafood and prime rib. "I think one of our main attractions is we appeal to a lot of different tastes in a very comfortable atmosphere," Howell said. OB's menu provides lots of options (with some Irish touches revealing OB's pub roots.) For lunch, there's everything from Truckee Chili (1984 winner of the annual Truckee Chili Cookoff) to Greek Pasta, a fettuccini topped with feta and Parmesan, tomatoes, and sautéed red and green peppers, eggplant and zucchini.

Burgers and classic sandwiches make an appearance, along with Mexican fare like Quesadillas, Fajitas and Tostadas. Salads include Caesar and Cashew Chicken Salad Mandarin, with chicken salad, greens, cashews, alfalfa sprouts, mandarin oranges, tomatoes and cucumbers. Lunches average $6.50. Portions are ample, and the service the fastest encountered in recent memory.

Wide-ranging dinner choices include Braised Swordfish with fresh pineapple, ginger, tomatillo salsa; Prime Rib in "Irish Cut" or "Leprechaun Cut"; Stuffed Breast of Chicken baked with brie, fresh basil and herbs, topped with bordelaise sauce; Grilled Pork Tenderloin marinated in garlic, olive oil, peppercorns and herbs, served with "OB's Fresh Santa Fe Salsa."

Dinners, served with French bread, homemade soup or salad—or Caesar Salad—baked potato, rice pilaf, or "steak fries" average $14.95.

Items can also be ordered from the "Pub Menu" for a one-course meal such as OB's best-selling Pasta Pacifica (fettuccini topped with shrimp, scallops and crab in a light cream sauce with Parmesan) or Crisp 'N Warm Won Ton Salad, a composite of stir-fried chicken, vegetables and peanuts with fried won ton wrappers on greens.

If you just want a snack, OB's has the kind of shared appetizers friends can munch on while downing a couple of cold ones. Among the options: Italian Bruschetta (French bread covered with sun-dried tomato, pesto, melted mozzarella and black olives), Irish Popcorn Shrimp (batter-fried petite shrimp served with cocktail and tartar sauces), and both traditional and Irish (potato skins with bacon, cheese, scallions and sour cream) Nachos. Prices average about $5.50.

The normal mix of business people and tourists one finds at OB's gives way to a throng of locals four times a year for parties worth crashing: Pray For Snow Party the first Thursday in November, Hawaiian Night on the last Thursday in January, St. Patrick's Day on March 17 and Cinco de Mayo. Drink specials, food specials and rock 'n roll, from 5 p.m. to 1 a.m. are featured.

PEEK AT THE PAST

An 1895 photo hanging on the wall at OB's shows townspeople shoveling out from a storm that dumped roof-deep snow on the town. The location of the present OB's is easy to spot in the photo as a bakery and Wm. McDougald's Fountain Saloon, where the main attraction is plainly advertised on the front of the building: 5-cent beer.

Another undated photo on display shows the three businesses now amalgamated into OB's as a grocery store, hardware store and bakery.

The legacy of the bakery is an enormous oven. You can see the oven doors and old bakery implements at OB's, where the oven's interior has been remodeled into a pantry.

Dick Howell says the bar at OB's was a speakeasy called Roma's during the Depression. He speculates that the portion of the restaurant which was once a bakery may be one of Truckee's oldest structures.

OB's owner Dick Howell relaxes in his favorite restaurant.

OB's Crisp 'N Warm Wonton Salad
(By Mike Linnett, owner/chef)

2 wonton squares, cut in strips and deep fried
2 cups (approximately) mixed greens (red leaf,
 romaine, butter lettuce) washed, dried and
 torn in bite-size pieces
3 teaspoons olive oil
6 ounces chicken breast, marinated in teriyaki
 sauce and cut in strips
1/2 carrot, thinly sliced
1/2 stalk celery, thinly sliced
1/2 yellow onion, thinly sliced
4 ounces dry roasted peanuts
2 scallions, diced
Sesame Dressing (recipe follows)

Placed mixed greens on individual serving platter. Top with
the fried wontons. Heat olive oil in sauté pan, add chicken strips,
carrot, celery, onion and peanuts. When cooked, add 1 1/2 ounces
of sesame dressing and toss. Arrange on greens and wontons, and
garnish with scallions. Serve with additional dressing on the side
to spoon over salad to taste. (Serves one.)

OB's Sesame Dressing

1/2 cup rice vinegar
2 teaspoons soy sauce
2 teaspoons sesame oil
1 teaspoon lemon juice
1/8 teaspoon cayenne pepper

Beat in small bowl with whisk until blended.

OB's Garlic Soup
(By Mike Babb, chef)

Note: When I first read this recipe, I assumed that the quantity of garlic (a half a *pound*) was an error, or possibly a joke. A quick phone call to OB's confirmed that Mike Babb wasn't kidding. So I made the soup. It has a strong garlic flavor, as you'd expect. But, to my amazement, it's not an overwhelmingly garlicky flavor. It's a delicious, hearty soup with a surprising sweetness (from the cabbage?) Guests will be quite astonished when you feed them this soup, then reveal the quantity of garlic they've just eaten.

½ head red cabbage, thinly sliced
½ head green cabbage, thinly sliced
1 cup onion, thinly sliced
½ cup celery, bias cut
2 tablespoons cooking oil
½ pound garlic (about 3½ *whole bulbs* of garlic; a bulb yields about 18 good-sized cloves, plus a bunch of dinky ones, hardly worth the trouble of peeling. What you need here is about 63 decent-sized cloves, peeled)*
2 quarts chicken stock
1 cup canned tomatoes, drained and diced
1 tablespoon dry basil
1 tablespoon dry thyme
1 tablespoon caraway seeds
⅜ cup rice vinegar

Sauté cabbage, onion and celery in oil. Sauté about five minutes, then add ¼ pound garlic, finely chopped. Continue cooking about five more minutes. Add chicken stock, bring to a boil, simmer one hour. Add remaining garlic, coarsely chopped, tomatoes, basil, thyme and caraway seeds. Simmer one-half hour. Adjust seasonings and add rice wine vinegar and serve. (Serves six to eight.)

* Note: Since this recipe involves so much garlic, you'll save yourself a whole lot of time if you buy a jar (it comes in a one-pound size) of peeled garlic. Another timesaver is to chop the garlic in a miniature food processor, if you have one.)

OB's Sierra Lamb Stew
(By Kurt Steeber, chef)

Note: Kurt Steeber guarantees this stew will ". . . take the sting of a Sierra winter's day out of our fingers and toes." If it works in Truckee—often cited on the winter news as the coldest spot in California—it should thaw frostbite just about anywhere. "Though the recipe calls for some mildly hot peppers and spices, those ingredients can be diminished or totally omitted and the flavor of the stew will not be completely compromised," according to the chef.

1½ teaspoons turmeric
1½ teaspoons cayenne pepper
1½ teaspoons ground white pepper
1½ teaspoons ground ginger
½ teaspoon ground coriander
½ teaspoon cumin
½ teaspoon dried basil
4–6 pounds lamb (preferably leg), in bite-size chunks
¼ cup unsalted butter
2 cups onion, finely chopped
2 cups green bell pepper, finely chopped
1½ cups celery, finely chopped
1 cup tomatillos, finely chopped
½ cup jalapeños, seeded amd finely chopped
½ cup pasilla peppers, finely chopped
2 green apples, peeled, cored and cubed
1 teaspoon ground ginger
1 teaspoon cinnamon
1 teaspoon marjoram
1 teaspoon thyme
2 teaspoons dry mustard (or 1 tablespoon of Dijon mustard)
2 teaspoons cayenne pepper
2 cups raisins
1½ cups honey

**1 cup red wine vinegar
mashed potatoes with fennel as accompaniment**

Combine first seven spices and toss with lamb chunks to coat. Set aside.

Melt butter in a stew pot (use a pot which can go in your oven) and sauté onion, bell pepper, celery, tomatillos, peppers and apples until soft. Add remaining spices and mix thoroughly. Use a wooden spoon to blend in raisins and honey. Simmer until the honey has been absorbed by the vegetables. Add lamb and stir until the meat is slightly browned. Add vinegar and stir.

Cover tightly and cook in preheated 325-degree oven for 1½ hours. Check lamb for doneness by pulling a piece apart. The meat should shred into thin strands. Continue cooking if necessary, but not for more than another 45 minutes. Serve immediately with mashed potatoes flavored with fennel. (Serves six.)

**OB's chef Mike Barrett offers the
standard antidote to Truckee's winter.**

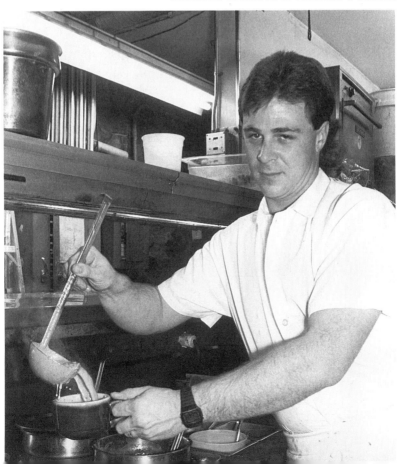

OB's Smoked Turkey and Lentil Soup

(By Mike Barrett, chef)

1½ cups dried lentils, rinsed and drained
6 cups boiling water
8 cups beef or chicken stock
6 ounces mushrooms, sliced
4 stalks celery, diced
3 carrots, diced
1 large onion, diced
1 teaspoon minced garlic
½ pound smoked turkey breast, diced
2 tablespoons fresh thyme, chopped
2 tablespoons fresh parsley, chopped
1 tablespoon fresh lime juice
¼ teaspoon grated lime peel
salt and pepper to taste

Place lentils in large pot. Cover with 6 cups boiling water. Let stand for two hours.

Drain lentils, return to pot. Add stock, vegetables and garlic and bring to a boil. Reduce heat to medium, cover and cook until lentils are soft, about one hour.

Mash to crush lentils, add turkey. Cook five minutes. Mix in herbs, lime juice and peel. Taste and add salt and pepper as needed. Serve immediately. (Serves eight to ten.)

OB's Spicy Peanut Chicken

(By Mike Babb, chef)

Note: Begin this recipe a day ahead—it marinates for 24 hours.

1 1/4 cups smooth peanut butter (unsalted)
3/4 cup soy sauce
1/4 cup brown sugar
1/3 cup water
1 1/4 teaspoon ground cinnamon
5 cloves garlic, minced
1/4 cup fresh lemon juice
1/2 teaspoon dried crushed red chiles
1/2 cup butter
3 onions, diced
8 8-ounce boneless chicken breasts

In a food processor, combine peanut butter, soy sauce, brown sugar, water, cinnamon, garlic, lemon juice and chiles. Transfer mixture to a saucepan over low heat. Add butter and melt, simmer for 5 minutes. Cool to room temperature.

Put onion and chicken breasts in a single layer in glass or plastic dish. Cover with marinade and marinate for 24 hours in refrigerator. Remove from refrigerator 1/2 hour before grilling.

Grill until done and serve. (Serves eight.)

THE PASSAGE

Corner of Commercial Row and Bridge Street, Truckee
☎ **(916) 587-7619**
Lunch: Monday–Saturday, 11:30 a.m.–3 p.m.;
Sunday, 10 a.m.–3 p.m.
Dinner: Monday–Thursday, 5:30 p.m.–10 p.m.;
Friday and Saturday, 5:30 p.m.–10:30 p.m.
(Slight seasonal variation in hours; if in doubt, call)
✌ **Reservations recommended**

Adventuresome food, friendly surroundings

LOCATED IN THE OLD TRUCKEE HOTEL, smack dab at the end of Commercial Row, The Passage is worth passing through for a delicious meal. Chef/owner Mark Baldwin and his wife Debora have been running the place since 1980, attempting to cater to the tastes of sophisticated skiers, summer campers, carbo-loading athletes and most of all, locals.

Baldwin gets a lot of inspiration from international sources, as reflected in his ever-changing daily specials. "Regardless of whether people can travel or not, they can vicariously travel and have adventures," he notes. Armchair travelers visiting The Passage might encounter appetizers like Tiger Prawns Stuffed with Feta, Goat Cheese and Roasted Red Peppers; Fresh Calamari Fritti with Tomato Creole Sauce; Wild Mushroom Raviolis; or Shrimp-Filled Artichokes. The average appetizer sets you back $5.95.

Lunch specials include items like Grilled Ahi with Papaya, Raspberry and Fig Relish with Wild Rice Pilaf as well as more humble burgers, salads (like the Greek Salad: greens with feta, Greek olives, tomatoes, cucumbers, dolmas, Greek peppers and onions); and sandwiches such as the Green Peppercorn Chicken Sandwich or the homemade Focaccia topped with eggplant, roasted red bell pepper, mozzarella and tomato sauce. Prices average around $6.50.

At dinner, look for homemade pasta du jour (i.e. Seafood Fettucini with Chinese Black Beans, Bok Choy, Red Bell Peppers and Mushrooms in an Oriental-style Sauce) and a meatless home-made Cannelloni. The "Mixed Grill" changes nightly, including components like Blackened Jumbo Prawns, Grilled Chicken Breast and Smoked Bratwurst with Dijonaise Sauce.

You'll find fresh fish specials every night, such as the Poached Salmon on Steamed Spinach with Tomato Béarnaise Sauce or Grilled Mahi Mahi served over Black Bean Chili with Papaya-Kiwi Salsa. More conventional fare (steaks, Smoked Cornish Game Hens) are also available. Entrées, served with steamed vegetables and red potatoes or wild rice pilaf, range from $10.95 to $17.95.

It's worth mentioning here that Mark smokes his own Cornish game hens, fish, and even vegetables (i.e. for his Smoked Tomato Chutney.) "Smoking is a good way to get a lot of flavor without adding calories," he says.

In addition, Mark likes "playing around with a lot of salsas" as an alternative to heavy use of butter and cream. "I like to use whatever's fresh. The focus is on fresh seasonal produce and seafood," he says.

A transplanted Easterner, he instituted the custom of "Lobster Night" in 1991 to boost business on slow Wednesdays. Flown in live from Maine, the lobsters were boiled and served with seafood salad or clam chowder for $16.95. We hope this tradition continues.

Desserts, prepared by The Passage's pastry chef, also change daily. Fresh Cranberry Crumb Tart, Chocolate-Espresso Mousse Pie, Fresh Raspberry Crème Brulee and Chocolate Pâté are the kinds of selections you can look forward to sampling.

Weekend brunch items include Eggs Benedict, Red Flannel Hash, Omelette du Jour, and Belgian Waffles topped with seasonal fruits.

PEEK AT THE PAST

Rob Sayers, who managed the Truckee Hotel from 1986 to 1989, shared some of his extensive research on the building which houses The Passage. Despite published accounts that the hotel opened in 1868, Sayers believes the business—originally named American House—opened in 1873. An ad dated August 27, 1873 in *The Truckee Republican* lists the price of board at $6 per week. "The house is new and pleasantly located convenient to the railroad and yet far enough to relieve lodgers of the unpleasantness caused by the noise of passing trains," according to the ad copy.

The first deed of sale is dated July 7, 1875, when Samuel McFarland sold the hotel to Stewart McKay.

An 1886 issue of *The Truckee Republican* contains an ad for the same business, known by then as the New American Hotel, with T. B. Whitney listed as proprietor. "Everything new . . . elegant rooms for families," the ad proclaimed. Board and lodging per week were available for $6 or $7, depending on the room, and single meals could be obtained for 25 cents. "The table will always be supplied with the best the market affords."

In 1909, the structure—by then known as Whitney House—burned to the ground, except the facade. A photo after the fire shows the facade with a sign: "Palace Grill, Lunchroom" on the front. Sayers said the fire, "was attributed to mice gnawing on matches in the linen closet." One man was killed attempting to escape from the burning building when he fell down a flight of stairs and broke his neck.

The hotel was rebuilt with miraculous speed, and an article announcing the grand opening of the New Whitney House appeared just 44 days after the fire.

The hotel changed hands and names many times over the years. It has been known as the Blume Hotel and the Riverside Hotel, and the word "Alpine" was added to make it Alpine Riverside Hotel for the 1960 Winter Olympics at Squaw Valley.

In 1976 Maryanne Boice and Stefanie Orozco renovated the building and changed the name to Truckee Hotel. Jeffrey and Karen Winter, who bought the hotel in 1991, reportedly plan a major restoration.

The Passage Baked Sea Bass on Bed of Curried Lentils with Tomato and Ginger Chutney

This is Mark Baldwin's three-part recipe. You'll want to make the chutney first, then the lentils, since the sea bass only takes a few minutes.

The Passage Tomato and Ginger Chutney

3 pounds plum tomatoes: peeled, seeded and
    quartered
1 4-inch-long piece of fresh ginger, cut in thin
    slices
8 medium garlic cloves
1 cup distilled white vinegar
1⅓ cups sugar
2 teaspoons salt
2 teaspoons sweet paprika
3 tablespoons fresh lemon juice
1 teaspoon cayenne pepper
2 teaspoons ground dried ginger
1 teaspoon dry mustard
¼ teaspoon ground cloves

Mix tomatoes and fresh ginger in a bowl; set aside. Purée garlic with ½ cup vinegar and pour into heavy non-aluminum pan. Mix in sugar and remaining ½ cup of vinegar. Cover and cook over medium heat until thickened, about 7 minutes. Add tomato mixture and all remaining ingredients. Bring to a boil, reduce heat to medium, and cook until thick, about 35 minutes. Mark says this recipe makes more than enough for 4–6 servings, and leftovers will keep for three weeks in the refrigerator. "Since it keeps so well, I always like to make a little extra. It's wonderful with chicken, also," he says.

The Passage Curried Lentils

1¼ cups lentils, picked over and rinsed
2 tablespoons vegetable oil
1 cup chopped onion
⅓ cup chopped red pepper
1½ teaspoons salt
1 teaspoon ground cumin
¾ teaspoon turmeric
½ teaspoon ground coriander
¼ teaspoon cinnamon
⅛ teaspoon cayenne pepper (adjust to taste)
⅛ teaspoon cloves

In a saucepan, combine lentils with 2½ cups water and bring to a boil. Cook over low heat 15 to 20 minutes or until barely tender. Put oil in a large skillet, add onion and red pepper and sauté until softened. Add spices and cook mixture for one minute. Add lentils and cooking liquid and simmer 10 minutes, stirring occasionally.

The Passage Baked Sea Bass

4 sea bass filets, about 8 ounces each
small amount of olive oil
salt and pepper

Rub filets with olive oil, then lightly salt and pepper them. Bake in a 400-degree oven until done, about 10–15 minutes, depending upon the size of filets. Serve on bed of Curried Lentils with Tomato and Ginger Chutney. (Serves four.)

The Passage Basque Steak

4 8–10-ounce top sirloins or New York steaks
12 strips bacon
1 yellow onion, peeled and diced
12 oysters, shucked; reserve oyster liquor
salt and pepper to taste

Charbroil steaks. Sauté bacon while the steaks are cooking. When bacon is done, remove and set aside. Pour off all but 1 tablespoon of bacon fat; cook onions in the same pan until translucent, then add the bacon, oysters, and oyster liquor. Oysters will cook quickly (1–2 minutes over high heat.) They're done when the meat firms up and the sides wrinkle.

"Butterfly" the steaks by using a sharp knife to cut a lengthwise pocket in the meat, taking care not to slice all the way through it. "You want something you can open up like a book," Mark says. (Don't cut through the fat, cut up to it.) Spoon portions of the filling in each steak. Fold steaks back over the filling and serve immediately. (Serves four.)

Mark and Debora Baldwin, owners of the Passage.

The Passage Grilled Salmon with Five Pepper Sauté and Herbed Polenta

Make and cool Mark Baldwin's Herbed Polenta before you begin the sauté and salmon (recipes on next page).

The Passage Herbed Polenta

3 cups milk
1 tablespoon unsalted butter
1 cup polenta (coarsely ground cornmeal)
1 teaspoon sugar
½ teaspoon salt
½ cup minced fresh herbs: basil, parsley, dill, chives or a mixture of whatever you have available
¼ cup grated Parmesan
2 tablespoons olive oil

Heat milk, butter, salt and sugar in large pot. When mixture is hot, but before it boils, add polenta in a slow but steady stream, stirring constantly with a wooden spoon. Lower the heat and continue cooking, stirring, until the polenta thickens and pulls away from the sides of the pot. Add herbs and Parmesan and stir to mix. Rub olive oil on a baking dish, then pour in polenta. Smooth it out with the spoon and let it cool.

Once the polenta has "set up" (which it does when it cools), it can be cut into different shapes with a knife or cookie cutter and baked, fried, deep fried or heated in a microwave. This recipe makes more than enough for the salmon dish on the next page. Mark says leftovers keep well in the refrigerator.

The Passage Five-Pepper Sauté

2 tablespoons olive oil, plus small additional
    amount for rubbing salmon
2 tablespoons minced shallots
2 tablespoons minced garlic
1/4 red bell pepper, seeded and cut into strips
1/4 green bell pepper, seeded and cut into strips
1/4 yellow bell pepper, seeded and cut into strips
1/2 Anaheim pepper, seeded and cut into strips
1 Jalapeño pepper, seeded and deribbed, diced
1 teaspoon dried thyme, crumbled
2 tablespoons dry white wine
1 cup clam broth

Heat a large sauté pan and add olive oil, then the garlic and shallots. Then add peppers and sauté over high heat, stirring frequently, until peppers start to soften. Add remaining ingredients (except salmon, salt and pepper), lower heat to a simmer, cover, and cook for 10–15 minutes.

While sauté is cooking, cut polenta (see recipe on previous page) into slices or other desired shapes and bake for 8–10 minutes in a 350-degree oven.

4 salmon filets (7–8 ounces each)
salt and pepper

When polenta and sauté are cooking, rub the salmon with olive oil, lightly salt and pepper, and then grill (or broil) until done.

Serve salmon on top of polenta. Spoon the pepper mixture and juice over both salmon and polenta. (Serves four.)

The Passage Linguini with Clams, Italian Sausage and Roma Tomatoes

1 pound linguini, fresh or dried, cooked al
    dente in 1 gallon of lightly salted water
40 small fresh clams (or substitute New Zealand
    cockles or mussels)
4 links Italian sausage, hot or mild
1/4 cup white wine
1 cup clam broth
2 tablespoons minced garlic
2 tablespoons minced shallots
1/4 cup heavy cream
4 roma tomatoes, peeled, seeded and diced
1/2 bunch fresh basil, minced, with 4 nice tops
    reserved for garnish
salt and pepper to taste

Soak clams in cold water for 10–15 minutes. While clams soak, poach sausage in saucepan containing 1/4-inch boiling water. Cover and cook sausages 5–7 minutes, then remove cover and brown sausages in same pan. Remove sausages and cut into coin-shaped slices. Put clams in large sauté pan with wine and clam broth. Cover and cook over high heat until clams open.

Remove clams to a bowl and strain the cooking fluid through a sieve lined with cheesecloth to remove any sand. Put the strained cooking liquid in a large sauté pan, add garlic and shallots and reduce by half. Add sausage slices and cream to sauté pan and reduce further. Finally add clams and any broth in the bowl, tomatoes, and minced basil; cook for an additional 1–2 minutes. Add salt and pepper to taste. Add the cooked noodles to the clam sauce and stir well, coating the noodles. Turn off heat and cover; let it sit for a few minutes before serving. Garnish with basil tops. (Serves four.)

The Passage Prawns Scampi Style with Artichoke Hearts

24 prawns, peeled and deveined, but with tail
 still intact (Mark uses a size which yields
 16–20 prawns per pound)*
2 tablespoons olive oil
2 tablespoons minced garlic
2 teaspoons minced shallots
3 tablespoons white wine
3 tablespoons clam broth or fish or shrimp stock
2 tablespoons heavy cream
1 tablespoon unsalted butter
juice of 1 lemon
12 artichoke hearts, halved (if canned, not the
 marinated type)
salt and pepper to taste

Sauté the prawns in olive oil over high heat. Watch them closely and remove when they turn pink. Place prawns in a bowl. Add garlic and shallots to the hot pan, stirring, then add the wine and clam broth or stock. Continue cooking until mixture reduces slightly, then add cream and butter and reduce further. Add the artichokes and cook for a minute. Add lemon juice and salt and pepper to taste. Finally, add the shrimp and any juices which have collected in the bowl. Serve as soon as shrimp is warmed, arranging the shrimp around the perimeter of each plate, with artichoke hearts and sauce in the middle. (Serves four.*)

*Note: As a main course, which should be served with rice to soak up any stray sauce. At The Passage, they also serve 3–4 prawns prepared this way with sliced bread (for sauce mopping) as an appetizer.

The Passage Shrimp-Filled Artichokes

4 artichokes, washed, with the tops of the leaves
   trimmed off with scissors
1¼ cups mayonnaise
1¼ cups grated Swiss cheese
1¼ cups bay shrimp
¼ teaspoon dried basil, crumbled
¼ teaspoon dried oregano, crumbled
⅛ teaspoon dried lavender, crumbled
salt and pepper to taste

Steam artichokes until done (heart is just tender when poked with a fork.) Cool enough to handle. Remove inner leaves, and use your fingers or a spoon to scrape out the choke and hairs which are attached to the heart. (Your finished product will have outer leaves attached to the cleaned heart—like a bowl.) Mix remaining ingredients together by hand and stuff each cleaned-out artichoke with an equal amount of filling. Stand the filled artichokes in a baking pan containing one inch of water. Cover with foil and heat in a 350-degree oven for about 10 minutes, or until artichokes are completely heated.* (Serves four.)

Note: If you prefer to heat your stuffed artichokes in a micro-wave, Mark says you can stand the filled artichokes in a baking dish with the bottom covered with water. Wrap in plastic and prick several holes in the wrapping. Microwave for 6–8 minutes or until thoroughly heated.

ZINA'S

10292 Donner Pass Road, Truckee
☎ (916) 587-3494
Breakfast and lunch (dinners also on Wednesday through Saturday):
Monday–Tuesday, 7 a.m.–6 p.m.;
Wednesday–Thursday, 7 a.m.–8 p.m.;
Friday, 7 a.m.–11 p.m.; Saturday 8 a.m.–11 p.m.;
Sunday, 8 a.m.–6 p.m.
(If in doubt, call ahead)
✌ Reservations recommended for dinner

Memorably unique

N O MATTER HOW MUCH of a dolt you are in terms of architecture, it's difficult to ignore the fact that Zina's is in an old, good-looking building. Located about an eighth of a mile west of downtown's Commercial Row, it turns out that Zina's is in the C. B. White House, a restored Queen Anne Eastlake-style Victorian listed on the National Register of Historic Places.

While this could make you wonder if you're about to get into something stodgy, forget it. The minute you walk in, the Victorian restoration takes a back seat to the pervasive atmosphere of eclectic whimsy. Zina's is alive with plants and bric-a-brac, casual conversation and aromas designed to derail your diet, especially if you've got a sweet tooth. "I want people to feel at home, comfortable, like they can meet their friends here, and they do," says owner Zina Krakowsky.

Her food, like her restaurant, is a marriage of fun and beauty. This directly reflects Zina herself, who's part finicky chef, part jazz dancer. Her customers benefit from both sides of the equation, and Truckee locals have enjoyed her imaginative meals and catering for over 20 years. (Zina and her former husband started OB's in 1970.)

She looks at food like an artist, because that's what she is. (If you think this sounds a bit pretentious, check out her photo album of wedding cakes and catering projects, best described as food sculpture.) "I relate to food in a number of different ways, as an art medium. I'm very conscious of color, texture and form. I don't believe in cutting the food up in little pieces and I don't purée very often."

Using her computer, Zina writes a new menu every day, changing items according to the weather, seasonal availability of fresh ingredients, and her abundant imagination.

Breakfasts get underway with fragrant coffee drinks and Zina's freshly-baked cakes, muffins, pies and surprises like a bowl made from croissant dough and filled with scrambled eggs, then baked.

Lunch items include things like Oriental Pasta Salad with chicken, vegetables, spicy peanut sauce and "Zinahair pasta," which turns out to be corkscrew curls. (You'll understand the reference immediately when you meet Zina.) Or you might find a strudel filled with smoked salmon, dill, mushrooms, onions, roasted peppers, artichoke hearts and Jarlsberg. Or a smoked turkey sandwich on coriander-laced sourdough bread with cream cheese and house apple raisin chutney, served with fresh fruit and berries.

Since the menu changes daily, you never know exactly what you'll find. This atmosphere of constant surprise is part of what makes Zina's fun. Vegetarians don't need to worry about finding choices here.

Lunch entrées average $6.25, many of them including salad. Dinners average $12.95 to $16.95, featuring items such as Pasta Pie (linguini with spinach, mushrooms, eggplant, artichoke hearts, sun-dried tomatoes, roasted red bell peppers, Monterey jack and Montrachet goat cheese in an herb-laced pastry shell), Beef Wellington, and lots of fresh seafood specials, each with a special sauce. Entrées are served with interesting vegetables such as sliced roasted eggplant and half a purple potato.

"When people go out to dine, it's a special occasion and they pay hard-earned money for it. I'm not here to fill people's stomachs—I'm here to give them an experience," Zina says.

Her rightfully famous desserts include items like Chocolate Delirium, Bohemian Poppy Seed Cake and Date Nut Torte.

Everything is fresh and homemade here—get ready to lick your plate. In summer, you can munch giant salads and other remarkable offerings outside on Zina's patio. (A good vantage point if a train goes by.) There's live music Fridays and Saturdays, of the accoustic variety, to accompany your dinner.

If you like Zina's recipes offered here, watch your bookstores. Zina has plans for her own cookbook.

PEEK AT THE PAST

The C. B. White house was built in about 1873 by William Henry Kruger, a partner in the successful Truckee Lumber Company. A native of Germany, Kruger lived in Grass Valley and Dutch Flat—working in mining, mercantile and sawmill businesses—before moving to Truckee with his wife and six children. He reportedly imported 14 craftsmen from Austria to build the home. When he died, in 1891, he left a fortune estimated at one million dollars.

Mary Adella Richardson Kruger, his widow, sold the home in 1904 to Charles Bernard White, a Bank of America executive. His wife, appropriately named Belle, was a former Sacramento beauty queen and a concert pianist. The piano lessons she offered in the home for decades are still remembered by some Truckee old-timers.

From about 1912 until the late 1920s, the White family operated the "White House Hotel" in their home, catering to the first automobile traffic over Donner Summit. Afterward, it returned to use as a family home, eventually suffering a period of vacancy and deterioration.

Restoring the building took more than seven years. Zina first opened a restaurant (called "C. B. White's") on this site in 1980. At this writing, it's the only building in Truckee listed in the National Register of Historic Places.

Zina's Blueberry Cardamom Muffins

1¼ cups all purpose flour
½ cup whole wheat flour
⅓ cup sugar
1½ teaspoons baking powder
⅛ teaspoon ground cardamom
3 tablespoons butter
¾ cup milk
½ teaspoon grated lemon rind
1 egg
½ teaspoon vanilla
1 basket fresh blueberries, washed and drained

Mix flours, sugar, baking powder and cardamom in mixing bowl. Cut in butter with a pastry blender. In a separate bowl, combine milk, lemon rind, egg and vanilla. Add wet mixture to dry ingredients, stirring until well combined. Fill muffin tins half full, then put six berries into the center of each muffin-to-be.

Cover with remaining batter, then add six more berries to the top of each. (Zina uses this method to avoid "streaking" caused by squished berries releasing juice when you stir them into the batter. It's a little more time-consuming, but you end up with very pretty muffins. If you happen to have children the right age, they would probably love the berry placement job.) Bake at 350 degrees for 15–20 minutes. (Makes one dozen.)

Zina's Bohemian Poppy Seed Cake

2¼ cups sifted flour
4 teaspoons baking powder
1½ cups sugar
½ cup butter
2 teaspoons vanilla
¾ cup poppy seeds
1¼ cups milk
3 egg whites
¼ teaspoon cream of tartar
2 tablespoons butter
¼ cup sliced almonds, toasted

Sift together flour and baking powder and set aside. In a large mixing bowl, cream together the sugar, butter and vanilla. Add the poppy seeds and mix well, scraping the sides and bottom of the bowl several times to thoroughly incorporate seeds. Add flour mixture to the sugar/butter mixture alternately with milk, stirring to blend after each addition. Beat egg whites with cream of tartar until they form stiff peaks, then fold into cake batter. Rub butter on inside of cake pan and shake almonds around to coat the pan. Add batter. Bake in a 350-degree oven for 30 minutes or until done.

Zina's: great food in a restored mansion.

Zina's Cardamom Coffeecake

2 cups butter, softened

2 cups brown sugar

4 eggs

2 teaspoons vanilla

2 cups sour cream

4 cups flour

2 teaspoons baking powder

2½ teaspoons baking soda

1½ teaspoons ground cardamom

½ teaspoon salt

Nut mixture:

¼ cup brown sugar

1 tablespoon cinnamon

½ cup pecan halves or large pieces, toasted on
cookie sheet in 350-degree oven for 10
minutes, then cooled

In a large mixing bowl, cream butter and sugar until light and fluffy. Beat 4 eggs and add to butter/sugar. Add vanilla and mix. In a separate bowl, mix flour, baking powder, baking soda, cardamom and salt. Add flour mixture to butter mix alternately with the sour cream, stirring after each addition to blend. Prepare nut mixture by hand. Spoon one-third of the cake batter into a buttered pan, then add one-third of the nut mixture, and continue until both components are used up, ending with a layer of nuts on top. Bake at 350 degrees for about one hour.

Zina's Carrot and Orange Soup

¾ pound carrots (about 3 medium-sized carrots)
3 tablespoons butter
2 medium onions, sliced
1 quart stock
2 large oranges, 1 peeled with peel reserved for
    garnish; both squeezed and juice strained to
    remove seeds.
1 teaspoon dried tarragon (optional)
¼ cup heavy cream

Melt butter in soup pot. Stir in carrots and onions, cover pan and let vegetables sweat over medium heat for 5 minutes. Pour in stock, bring to a boil, reduce heat and simmer, covered, 15 minutes. Purée the vegetables and stock. Add orange juice and purée again. Add tarragon if desired. Return to pot, add cream, reheat without boiling. Cut orange peel into slivers. Simmer peel in water 5 minutes, drain and use as garnish. (Serves three.)

Zina's Cream of Watercress Soup

¼ cup sweet butter
1 large onion, chopped
2 stalks celery, sliced
1 small leek, sliced
4 potatoes, diced
6 cups chicken broth
2 cups watercress leaves, plus extra for garnish
2 cups light cream
salt and pepper to taste

Melt butter in soup pot. Add onion, celery and leek and sauté until soft. Add potatoes and broth. Simmer until potatoes are soft. Add watercress leaves, stir, and cool the soup slightly, then purée. Stir in light cream just before serving, adding salt and pepper to taste. Serve chilled or warm, garnished with watercress sprigs. ("I use the ones with flowers," Zina says.) (Serves eight to ten.)

Zina's Date Bars

1 pound pitted dates, cut up
½ cup water
1 lemon, seeded and cut in 5 or 6 pieces
1 orange, seeded and cut in 5 or 6 pieces
1 cup sugar or 2/3 cup honey (both optional)
1½ cups rolled oats
¾ cup white flour
¾ cup whole wheat flour
½ teaspoon baking soda
1 cup walnut pieces
1 teaspoon cinnamon
1 cup brown sugar
1 cup butter, melted

Simmer the dates. water, lemon, orange, sugar or honey (if desired) in a saucepan until dates become smooth. Add more water if necessary to keep mixture from scorching. Cool. Remove orange and lemon. You can cut up the peels and incorporate if you like. Set aside.

Mix oats, flours, baking soda, walnuts, cinnamon and brown sugar well in a mixing bowl. Then stir in butter.

Pat half the oat mixture into an 8-inch by 8-inch buttered pan. Spread with date filling. Pat remaining oat mixture over filling. Sprinkle top with cinnamon, if desired.

Bake at 325 degrees for 30–45 minutes, until lightly browned. Cut while warm. (Makes 16 2-inch squares.)

Zina's Date Nut Torte

6 egg whites

¼ teaspoon cream of tartar

½ cup honey

10 ounces diced dates

3 cups finely chopped toasted walnuts, almonds
  or hazelnuts

2 tablespoons finely chopped orange zest, plus
  extra for decoration

1 tablespoon Grand Marnier

For glaze:

1 teaspoon unflavored gelatin

1 tablespoon Grand Marnier

½ cup raspberry preserves (seedless)

Using an electric mixer, beat egg whites with cream of tartar until peaks just begin to form. Drizzle in honey and continue beating until stiff. Carefully fold the dates, nuts, orange zest and Grand Marnier into the meringue. Spread meringue in a prepared (either lined with parchment or oiled and floured) 9-inch cake pan. Bake in a 325-degree oven approximately 35 minutes. Cool and apply glaze with pastry brush. Decorate with orange zest.

To make glaze, place gelatin in a small glass bowl, add Grand Marnier and stir. Heat a few seconds in the microwave, until it bubbles. Stir. Make sure gelatin granules have dissolved. Add preserves a little at a time, stirring constantly.

Alternately, if you don't have a microwave oven, heat preserves over low heat and stir in Grand Marnier, omitting gelatin.

Zina's Dutch Pancakes

Note: These creep up the sides of the pan as you bake them, so choose a pan with fairly tall sides.

1/2 cup melted clarified butter
5 eggs
1 cup milk
1 cup flour
2 teaspoons sugar
fruit preserves or maple syrup

Preheat oven to 375 degrees. Ladle butter into baking dish, roll to coat sides, place dish in oven to heat. Mix eggs and milk in blender. Add flour and sugar to egg mixture while continuing to blend. Pour batter into center of melted butter in hot dish. Bake 12 to 15 minutes. Serve topped with fruit preserves or maple syrup. (Serves two.)

Zina's (Flourless) Nut Torte

4 eggs, separated
1/4 cup honey
1 teaspoon vanilla extract
1 teaspoon almond extract
1/2 teaspoon nutmeg
3/4 teaspoon cinnamon
2 cups ground almonds
1/8 teaspoon cream of tartar
raspberry jelly for glaze (approximately 1/2 cup)

Beat egg yolks using an electric mixer at high speed until yolks become very thick. Slowly drizzle in honey, then lower speed. Add extracts, nutmeg and cinnamon and mix. Fold in almonds, set aside. Whip egg whites with cream of tartar until stiff but not dry. Fold 1/3 of whites into yolk mixture, then fold in the rest of the whites. Spread in oiled or buttered bundt (or other) pan and bake at 350 degrees until barely done—test at 45 minutes. Do not overbake or the cake will become dry. Cool. Use a pastry brush to apply melted raspberry jelly as a glaze.

Zina's Fresh Pear Cake

1 cup sugar
½ cup butter
2 eggs
2 cups flour
2 teaspoons baking soda
2 teaspoons cinnamon
½ teaspoon nutmeg
2 teaspoons vanilla
¼ cup sherry
4 cups chopped pears
1 cup pecans, toasted

For glaze:

½ cup powdered sugar
2 tablespoons sherry

Cream sugar and butter together in large mixing bowl, add eggs. In a separate bowl, sift together flour, baking soda, cinnamon and nutmeg. Mix well and add to sugar/butter/eggs. Add vanilla and sherry. Fold in pears and pecans. Bake in buttered bundt pan at 325 degrees for one hour or until done. Cool. Mix glaze and drizzle on top.

**On her menu, Zina Krakowsky advises
customers to eat dessert first.**

Zina's Middle Eastern Lamb-Stuffed Zucchini

2 teaspoons olive oil
½ onion, chopped fine
1 clove garlic, minced
1 small red bell pepper, minced
¼ cup bulgur
⅓ cup currants
½ teaspoon allspice
¼ teaspoon cinnamon
pepper to taste
½ pound finely chopped lean lamb
4 zucchini, 1½ inch diameter, scrubbed, cut
    in half lengthwise and hollowed out to make
    each half into a container
Mint Yogurt Sauce (recipe follows)

Heat oil and sauté onion, garlic and pepper until soft, remove from heat. Stir in bulgur, currants, allspice, cinnamon and pepper. Cool and transfer to large bowl. Add lamb and combine well. Divide lamb mixture and stuff into zucchini. Place a rack in a rectangular pan (about 3 inches deep) and add about 1 inch of hot water. Put stuffed zucchini halves back together, arranging them on rack. Cover pan with metal lid or foil. Place in a 350-degree oven and steam over simmering water, covered, for about one hour. Slice in ½-inch diagonal slices and serve hot, room temperature, or cold with Mint Yogurt Sauce. (Serves four to six.)

Zina's Mint Yogurt Sauce

1 cup plain yogurt
½ cup grated cucumber
2 tablespoons minced fresh mint
    (or 1 teaspoon dried)

Combine ingredients and serve with Middle Eastern Lamb-Stuffed Zucchini.

Zina's Nepal-Style Chicken Curry

"Awesome"—Zina

1/4 cup oil
1 large onion, sliced
12 whole garlic cloves
2 tablespoons minced fresh ginger
2-inch stick cinnamon
2 whole cardamom, shells removed
1 large tomato, peeled and cut in eighths
1 tablespoon ground coriander
1 tablespoon shredded unsweetened coconut
1 1/2 teaspoons ground cumin
1 cut-up broiler/fryer chicken
    (about 3 1/2 pounds)
1/2 cup double-strength chicken stock
pinch of saffron
1 tablespoon salted roasted cashews
1 tablespoon raisins or currants
2 hard-cooked eggs, sliced, for garnish
1 bunch fresh coriander leaves (cilantro)
    for garnish

Heat oil over medium high heat in heavy frying pan. Add onion, garlic, ginger, cinnamon and cardamom. Cook, stirring, for about 5 minutes, until onion is browned. Add tomato and cook until liquid evaporates. Add ground coriander, coconut, cumin, chicken and stock. Cover and simmer until meat is done, about 45 minutes. Transfer meat to serving dish. Add saffron, cashews and raisins or currants to sauce and boil until reduced to one cup. Skim and discard fat. Pour sauce over chicken and serve, garnished with coriander and eggs. (Serves four.)

Zina's Persimmon Patties

1 cup walnuts, almonds, pecans, hazelnuts or
   combination
1 1/2 cups unsweetened shredded coconut
1 1/2 cups pitted dates
2 cups currants
1 teaspoon cinnamon
1/2 teaspoon cloves
1/2 teaspoon mace
1/2 teaspoon nutmeg
1 teaspoon vanilla extract
2 tablespoons grated orange rind
3 cups graham cracker crumbs
1 cup persimmon pulp
extra graham cracker crumbs or coconut
   for rolling cookies in

Chop nuts, coconut, dates, and currants in food processor until combined, but still chunky. Transfer to mixing bowl. Add remaining ingredients. Form into one-inch balls and roll in graham cracker crumbs or coconut, then flatten. Serve. (No cooking!) Makes about five dozen. These can be kept in the refrigerator for several days, according to Zina, and extras freeze well.

Zina's White Chocolate Almond Cake

8 ounces white chocolate
4 ounces unsalted butter, softened
1 cup granulated sugar
8 eggs, separated
6 tablespoons crème de cacao
1 cup ground blanched almonds
1/2 teaspoon baking powder
1/2 cup flour
1 cup graham cracker crumbs
8 eggs whites
1/4 teaspoon cream of tartar

For glaze:

1/2 cup powdered sugar
enough Amaretto to make a drippy consistency

In a large mixing bowl, cream sugar and butter together until fluffy. Add yolks, one at a time, beating after each. Beat until mixture is thick. Add crème de cacao. Melt chocolate over hot water in double boiler (or in microwave oven.) Blend melted chocolate into mixture. In another bowl, mix almonds, baking powder, flour and graham cracker crumbs. Fold dry mixture into chocolate mixture and set aside. Whip egg whites and cream of tartar until stiff but not dry. Fold one-third of egg whites into chocolate mixture, then fold in remainder and smooth into prepared bundt pan. Bake in a 350-degree oven for approximately 30 minutes.

When cool, invert cake on serving plate. Combine glaze ingredients and drip over cake.

Index

134

137